Women Married
to Alcoholics

WOMEN MARRIED TO ALCOHOLICS

Help and Hope for Nonalcoholic Partners

Morris Kokin with Ian Walker

William Morrow and Company, Inc.   *New York*

Library of Congress Cataloging-in-Publication Data

Kokin, Morris.
Women married to alcoholics.

1. Co-dependence (Psychology)   2. Alcoholics—Family
relationships.   3. Wives—Mental health.   I. Walker,
Ian (Ian Frank)   II. Title.
RC569.5.C63K65   1989   362.29′23   89-8248
ISBN 0-688-08154-1

Printed in the United States of America

First Edition

1 2 3 4 5 6 7 8 9 10

BOOK DESIGN BY KARIN BATTEN

To my beloved parents, Helen and Leon, who taught me the value of life, the meaningfulness of suffering, and the importance of going on; and to my sister, Eta, and my brother, Fred, whose love and companionship will forever be a vital part of my life

M.K.

To my mother, Gladys Walker, a constant source of strength and encouragement

I.W.

Preface

A close friend of mine married a bright, handsome, charming man, they had three children, and then he started coming home drunk every day. During the years that she stuck by him, as he lost one job after another and embarrassed both her and the children countless times, our mutual acquaintances told me, "There must be something wrong with her, or she wouldn't stay with him. She seems nice, but she must be doing something to make him drink." In fact, she stayed with him because in many other respects he was a fine man and a good father. She had tried hard to help him in various ways, she didn't want to "deprive the children of their father," and she had been taught that a good woman stands by her man.

When he lost his fourth job in as many years and had depleted the entire family savings through his alcoholism, she took the children and left. In a telephone call, he said bitterly to her, "Boy, when the going got tough, you just took off." What was worse, many of her alleged friends said, "There must have been *something* more you could have tried."

As Morris Kokin says, "It is one thing to have to live with an alcoholic, but to be accused of causing or supporting his drinking must be the height of injustice." And then, when you *do* leave, to be accused of letting your husband down, of being a bad or selfish woman, adds painful insult to injury. Nevertheless, this is exactly what our society, egged on and legitimized by most mental health professionals, does to women who are involved with alcoholics. This attitude is puzzling, because, as Kokin points out, the expert professionals find it often difficult to diagnose and usually difficult to treat alcoholism, yet we expect women to be able to recognize alcoholism in their husbands and to know how to get them to stop drinking.

When my book *The Myth of Women's Masochism* was published, I was astounded to find that so many people who easily saw my basic point—*that women do not enjoy their suffering*—nonetheless continued to say that wives of alcoholics were "codependents," that they enabled their partner to keep on drinking, and that they somehow "needed" to be miserable. In trying to understand why they made this massive exception, I came to these conclusions:

1. Believing women are codependents takes the focus off the alcoholic himself, and that's a relief, because alcoholism is so hard to treat and the recovery rate is so low.
2. It allows one to blame women for yet another problem, and women-blaming in our culture is a widely accepted activity.
3. The theorists of codependency created a whole new set of jargon and counterintuitive principles, and this gives perplexed, frustrated professionals a sense of control, power, and efficacy as they speak a new language that ordinary people cannot understand.

Treating women partners of alcoholics as though they are the villains or as though they enjoy their men's alcoholism or both makes women feel sick, powerless, and hopeless. Morris Kokin's approach is a commonsense, jargon-free one that empowers women by depathologizing them, by saying what women in such positions *can* do for themselves and their children, and by courageously (how shocking that this takes courage!) pointing out that a man's alcoholism and the damage it does is *his own* responsibility.

Kokin is a pioneer in what I hope will become a torrent of writing in which women who do their best to cope in the face of adversity are seen not as enjoying and feeding the trouble but as being trapped and, in spite of that, drawing on what strength and creativity they can muster. Such people, when male, are usually called heroes, not codependents.

This book should be read not only by women partners of alcoholics but by alcoholics themselves, the professionals who work with them, and by children of alcoholics. It is useful also for women living with people who have a variety of addictions including drug abuse and compulsive gambling or womanizing, and indeed for women in any miserable intimate relationship—such as with a batterer or a partner who compulsively denies and avoids dealing with problems in the relationship.

—Paula J. Caplan, Ph.D.

Acknowledgments ▬▬▬▬▬▬▬▬▬

Many people contributed directly and indirectly to the completion of this book, and the authors wish to express their heartfelt gratitude to all. A special thanks goes to our literary agent, Bella Pomer, for her wonderful supportiveness throughout the project. Further thanks goes to James Landis, our publisher, whose infectious enthusiasm from the outset provided vital encouragement. Thanks most of all, however, must go to the many women who shared both time and candor in discussing the issues raised in this book; though anonymous, you know who you are, and you know that our appreciation runs deep.

Morris Kokin: First and foremost, I wish to thank my dear wife, Eileen, without whose love, patience, understanding, and constant encouragement I could never have completed this work. Additional thanks to my dear friends Connie Peacock and Alan Tanny, who devoted many hours to reviewing the material and whose advice helped shape the final manuscript. Thanks also to Dr. Dollard Cormier, Dr. Germain Lavoie, and Dr. John Wright at the University of Montreal for helping me develop my ideas and encouraging me to pursue my beliefs; to Dr. Sol Levine, vice-president of the Henry J. Kaiser Foundation, who provided me with much-needed support and friendly guidance; to Dr. Ahmed Fayek, teacher, mentor, and dear friend, who taught me how to look beyond the obvious and how to hear and understand the silence; and to Lorraine McCullough, director general of Foster Clinic in Montreal, for creating an environment that has always encouraged further learning and has discouraged complacency. I would also like to thank friends and staff at Foster who not only put up with me through a difficult year, but also provided support, guidance, and valuable ideas. My ultimate thanks, however, go to my patients, whose strength, courage, and perseverance in the face of immense pain and suffering have touched my soul and taught me the meaning of humility. Your lives, your experiences, your pride, courage, and dignity are the essential seeds that gave birth to this book.

Ian Walker: The first person I wish to thank is Carole Dupuy, a great lady and one of the truly special people in my life, for reasons we both know. A further thanks to her sister, Nicole, a psychoeducator who shared valuable insights as the manuscript progressed. I would also like to thank librarian Joanne Head, whose information skills were most helpful. Other thanks go to Kevin Walker, who reviewed the manuscript from start to finish and provided frequent research assistance. Thanks also to Christiane Lafortune for her help and advice.

Contents

To the Reader: A Note on Usage

Women Married to Alcoholics is intended to help anyone who is or has been involved with the issue of alcoholism. It is especially intended for all those women who are or once were involved in an intimate relationship with an alcoholic man. The word *married* in the title is used in its broadest dictionary sense, "to enter into a close or permanent union." Thus, the word *wives* includes common-law wives, girlfriends, and live-in companions.

Introduction ■■■■■■■■■■

This book is about women who fall in love with men who are in love with alcohol. It is the story of men who are hooked on drinking and the women who are hooked on these men. It is a story about trust and betrayal, hostages and hostage takers, and about struggle for freedom and survival. It is also a story about an age-old love triangle: the woman, the man she loves, and his mistress—the bottle.

Who are these women? What happens to them during the years their mate is drinking? Why do they stay with him when he continues to drink, and what happens to them if he stops? These are some of the issues the book addresses. In doing so, it attempts to cast light on a shadowy and pervasive form of household terrorism that has long gone unchallenged. Are these women hostages, or are they willing accomplices? Are they victims or villains? How has society responded to their needs, and to what extent have our social systems failed them? What steps can be taken to improve or rectify the situation?

As we will see, the relationship between a woman and her alcoholic mate is a study in love and hate, pity and anger, fear and confusion. When we consider the findings of a recent Gallup poll that one family in four in the United States reports a problem with alcohol at home, it becomes clear that the potential for such relationships is frighteningly widespread. And when we realize that this figure represents a *100* percent increase over the findings of little more than a decade ago, the picture becomes even more grim.

Other figures are equally disturbing. While we now know that alcoholism strikes people in all walks of life, regardless of age, sex, or socioeconomic status, the sheer magnitude of the affliction suggests a problem of epidemic proportions. In the United States alone (using this country as a very broad model for what is going on elsewhere in the world), an estimated eighteen million* individuals suffer from some form of alcohol abuse. Add to this the commonly held notion that the problem drinker affects at least five other people in his or her circle, and the number of victims, direct and indirect, including

*A widely accepted figure. Other estimates, using the term "alcoholic," range from 9 to 22 million.

drinkers themselves, increases to well over 100 million, or more than a third of the national population.

At the core of this expanding nightmare are spouses and children. They are in many ways the hidden casualties of alcoholism. As an article in the November 30, 1987, issue of *Time* puts it, ". . . another shadowy fact of life about alcoholics has been dragged into the light: the severe emotional scars they leave on their spouses and especially on their children."

The word "especially" is revealing. No one would deny that the children have it bad—but why the traditional inference that spouses have it less so? One possible answer is that in our society it is somehow assumed that adults, unlike children, have the freedom to pick and choose and thus have power and control over their own destiny.

In this book we shall look at just how "free" wives of alcoholics really are.

Violence is a feature of many alcoholic households—indeed, of the alcoholic landscape in general. Almost a third of the half million state prison inmates in the United States drank heavily before committing crimes ranging from rape to assault. On the home front the story is similar. Of all family-court cases of violence between husband and wife, up to half are said to be the result of abusive drinking.

Even when a husband is not physically violent, the wife of an alcoholic suffers in countless emotional and psychological ways. As the consequences of alcohol abuse mount—as the alcoholic's behavior becomes more and more irresponsible and unpredictable—so do the wife's responses become increasingly inconsistent. One moment she is angrily confronting him, the next moment she is covering up for his behavior. One day she hates him and threatens to leave, the next day she is feeling guilty, blaming herself, and wondering what *she* can do to change.

Research on partners and children of alcoholics is still scanty. Although a great deal of attention has recently been focused on the effects of parental alcoholism on children and adult children, the technical literature concerning the effects on spouses remains sparse. What has been written is mainly about alcoholic men and their nonalcoholic wives. This may be partly because alcoholism was once thought to be almost exclusively a male problem. Linked to this is the fact that female alcoholics have tended to remain cloistered from society's view. As well, possibly for economic reasons, wives of alcoholics often stay in their marriage, while husbands of alcoholics usually leave. Certainly, in all of these areas, more research is required.

Even in the area of "family" therapy, the reality usually consists of treatment of an alcoholic man with the involvement, at some level, of his nonalcoholic wife. Typically, the wife is utilized as an adjunct to the husband's treatment. This is a little like giving Valium or Antabuse to the alcoholic, except in this case it is the wife that is being used as medication.

On the surface, the reasoning behind this appears sound. It has been found that a wife's involvement in the husband's treatment tends to benefit that treatment. But is that enough? Does successful treatment of the husband really mean the successful repair of an entire family broken—"like a doll's house," to quote one client—by this thing called alcoholism? Would we send home victims of a car crash, the husband attended to, the wife and children clutching in their hands their own bandages?

As if the anguish of living with an alcoholic were not enough, the wife of such a person may endure further indignity because of the way in which she is so often typecast. Various studies—which I shall look at in the book—have depicted wives of alcoholics as potentially villainous.

Even some of the terms that are commonly used hint in this direction. The wife or female partner of an alcoholic is referred to by such words as "enabler," "codependent," or "coalcoholic." These tags tend to suggest some complicity—the idea of an accomplice or co-conspirator who may have been responsible for the creation of her husband's drinking problem, or who, at the very least, may have cooperated with his desire not to stop drinking. While this was not necessarily the intent of such terms, they are nonetheless catchwords that have negative and misleading connotations.

The result of such labeling is all too often misjudgment and misunderstanding, however subtle or gross. In some instances, this has reached the point where the alcoholic himself is viewed as an innocent victim of a severely disturbed woman who has either driven him to the bottle or who has taken advantage of his illness for benefits of her own, and thus behaves in a manner compatible with keeping him where he is.

It is one thing to have to live with an alcoholic, but to be accused of causing or supporting his drinking must be the height of injustice. If it is the wife's suffering and her inability or lack of effort to get him to stop that has resulted in her being labeled an enabler, then do we not all fit this description? After all, society has also been paying a very heavy price for the consequences of alcoholic behavior, and our efforts to halt the situation have been just as fruitless. Every year thousands of us fall victim to drunk drivers. The newspapers bleed daily with stories of violent crimes committed by individuals too drunk to think twice. We pay out billions of dollars annually in treatment, rehabilitation, and medical care, as well as for lost time in industry.

While it is true that more treatment programs have opened up in recent years (in the United States there are more than seven thousand, a 65 percent increase in the past six years alone), the sad fact is that only a small portion—15 to 20 percent—of alcoholics actually do get treatment; and even then, the recovery rate is disturbingly low.

Yet despite such limited success in the professional domain, the wife continues to be held accountable. She is a convenient scapegoat, representing society as the one who is responsible for causing or maintaining the alcoholism of her husband. If alcoholism is a disease, how could the wife have given it to her husband? And if she is not the cause, what expertise and training is she supposed to have that would enable her to cure him of it? Our society possesses no known cure for this terrible affliction; why should the wife be expected to have some special ability in this area?

Even though women and children who live with chronic drinkers are the front-line casualties of alcoholism, far more has been written about the heavy cost of alcoholism to industry and community than about the cost to family. In the United States, the tab for alcohol-related absenteeism, lateness, poor judgment, errors, accidents, and accident benefits has been pegged at more than $100 billion a year.

If the price is so high for those who are at arm's length from the problem, let us imagine what the price must be for those closest. While we cannot put monetary figures on the situation faced by wives and children, we can readily surmise that the emotional cost—in terms of absenteeism, violence, unpredictability, erosion of trust, financial instability—must be at least as colossal. And, certainly, some of this cost to the children has already begun to filter through. Studies indicate a high percentage of involvement in juvenile delinquency and drug abuse. As well, children of alcoholics experience a greater frequency of marital difficulties in their own relationships as adults, and run a significant risk of becoming alcoholics themselves.

To what extent are the children's difficulties a by-product of the mother's own difficulties? It has been suggested that because wives of alcoholics are often forced to assume responsibilities and roles that would not have been necessary if their husbands were nonalcoholic, such women are so preoccupied with their partners' drinking that they are unable to interact with their children in a consistent and positive manner.

Certainly the "loss" of the mother is almost always noted by families, and is much of the time judged harshly. While the drinker may be seen as sick and his irresponsible behavior as due to drunkenness, she is seen as sober, supposedly clear-headed, and expected to do something about the situation. The father may recover and become the subject of well-deserved praise. But the mother? She did not suffer from alcoholism, she had no "ism" to recover from. What did she do, other than "permit" the disease to progress unchecked in her husband?

Jill, a daughter we will meet later in the book, emerged from just such circumstances. As she put it: "It took years before I was able to stop blaming my mother . . . before I was able to see that she too had been affected, that she too was hurting badly."

Jill's words underscore an essential premise of this book: that though not all women suffer in the same way or to the same degree, *any* woman who is engaged for a significant length of time in an alcoholic relationship will be somehow affected. And even when the partner stops drinking, the wife's acquired problems do not automatically disappear. Why this is so is what I seek to explain.

One of the hazards in writing a book of this nature, a book devoted primarily to the point of view of the wife, is of seeming to underrepresent the plight of the alcoholic himself. Regardless of my sympathies in the matter, however, I feel that this particular perspective has already been well served in scores of other books, some of which are listed at the back of this volume. Furthermore, I recognize that the true culprit in this book is alcoholism itself. The alcoholic, his partner, and children are *all* victims.

The alcoholic is the host of a cruel affliction, conceivably a disease, and his drinking frequently renders him out of control. The cost to such a person—in terms of physical health, mental and emotional functioning, and ability to interact with others—has been well documented. There are indications that alcoholism reduces life expectancy significantly and spawns numerous diseases affecting circulation, and gastrointestinal and neurological functioning. Cirrhosis of the liver claims thousands of alcoholics annually, and death from pneumonia is much commoner than for nonalcoholics.

Certain "bizarre" diseases also accompany excessive drinking. These range from polyneuropathy, which can result in permanent crippling, to the nightmarish condition known as Korsakoff's psychosis ("wet brain"), which results in irreversible brain damage. Suicide? It is a widely accepted fact that between 10 and 30 percent of all suicides are alcohol-related, and that a significant percentage of all alcoholics commit suicide.

Chilling as these few facts are, however, they only reinforce the necessity for this book. While we as a society look at the alcoholic, in some cases mesmerized by the sad and stunning irrationality of such a disease, by its apparent incurability, what often gets forgotten is the woman who stands beside the alcoholic. What about the wife who watches helplessly as her husband is dragged headlong into any of the above circumstances—into terminal unemployment, into cirrhosis, into Korsakoff's psychosis or suicide? What about the woman who is simply forced to leave (assuming she is able), having exhausted all avenues of assistance, because her husband has become so violently and miserably transformed by this abysmal disease?

These are just a few of the questions I raise and examine in this book. To say that I have all or even many of the answers would be naive. Just as alcoholism is a riddle, so too is the situation surrounding wives. To say that I may have some answers is closer to the truth. One thing is certain: I feel it is time more of us started asking questions. I feel it is time more of us started looking at a segment of society that has been cruelly, if unintentionally, neglected, misunderstood, and misjudged.

I feel, in fact, that the time is long overdue

M.K.

Women Married
to Alcoholics

One

When Dreams Go Wrong

... even if spouses do not abuse alcohol they can
come to resemble drunks, since their anger and fear
are enormous, way beyond what you'd find in a truly
sober person. . . .

—*Newsweek,* January 1988

A client once told me a dream she had had. In it she and her husband
and their two children were walking in a park. It was a beautiful day
and there were people all around, strolling on the grass, admiring the
flowers, setting out bright picnic cloths in the sunshine. She herself
felt particularly exhilarated, enjoying the happiness reflected on her
husband's and children's faces.

After several minutes they came to a small artificial lake, little more
than an outsized wading pond, and they rented a boat. Her husband
rowed while she and the children sat in the stern. He seemed very
pleased with himself, and with almost every other stroke of the oars
would smile at her. As the boat neared the center of the lake,
however, he grew restless. Standing up, he kicked off his shoes and
stripped off his shirt and, despite her protests, dived into the water.

The children thought this was fun. The wife, though, felt uneasy,
aware that something was wrong. Somehow the lake was bigger than
she had initially thought, the people on the shore were now very tiny,
and the sky had grown suddenly overcast. Then she spotted the
danger: There was a whirlpool near where her husband was swimming, and the whirlpool was growing wider and wider, threatening to

suck him in. Although she tried to scream a warning at him, no sound came from her mouth. Her husband merely paused to wave, then—seemingly oblivious—kept on swimming. Moments later he was caught by the current and was dragged, struggling, closer and closer to the eye of the whirlpool. By now the children were frightened and crying.

Panicky and yet still unable to scream, the wife stood up and threw a rope to her drowning husband. Miraculously, he caught it. But now, instead of being able to pull him out of the spinning maelstrom, she herself was being pulled into it—she, the boat, and the two children. The only thing to do, to save herself and the children, was to let go of the rope. But now the terror and confusion were so intense that her hands were frozen; they refused to let go. And now the boat was tipping into the vortex.

Throughout my years in practice I have often reflected on this dream. The reason is simple. Though it may lend itself to various other psychological interpretations, it very much symbolizes what happens in many alcoholic marriages. It is a nightmare that expresses the experience not just of the sad young woman who dreamed it but that of millions of anonymous women everywhere

BRIGHT SMILES, SILENT TEARS

Melanie, the woman who had this dream, was thirty-one when she first came to see me. Married eleven years, she had two sons, ages eight and nine. She was petite and innocent-looking, with very short blond hair and eyes that were blue and direct. She entered my office smiling cheerfully, her gaze warm and confident. I recall her appearance clearly because I remember thinking that though I was aware of her age, she seemed much younger. Her clothes were vivid and youthful, her lipstick bright, and her makeup somewhat over-done, like that of a child who has secretly experimented with her mother's cosmetic tray.

Melanie had been referred to me by her doctor following a number of medical tests over the past two years. Although she complained of recurring abdominal pains, there was no discernible cause—the symptoms seemed to evaporate as mysteriously as they arrived. Her doctor had finally suggested that the problem might be emotionally rooted and that she should consult a psychologist.

"So I guess that's why I'm here—because of my doctor," she said with an apologetic shrug. "And to tell the truth, I feel rather silly sitting in a psychologist's office. I'm sure you're a busy man, and I shouldn't be wasting your time."

When I pointed out that she seemed to be feeling like an intruder, Melanie paused for a few seconds, then smiled again and said: "I suppose I am. I'm really not too sure why I'm here or what to say."

"Maybe you can tell me a little about who you are."

"Well . . . what do you want to know?" She sounded mildly flustered. "I'm not certain where to start."

"Tell me whatever you think might be important for me to know—something that would help me understand who Melanie is."

She glanced slowly around the room, as though to assure herself that we really were alone and that it was safe to speak. For a moment or two her smile vanished and a flicker of sadness replaced it. She appeared to be deep in thought, but an instant later her composure was back and she was smiling again.

"There just isn't much to tell, really. I'm a pretty uncomplicated person—happily married, my husband has a good job and works hard, and we have two beautiful kids I love very much. We also have a nice home, a couple of cars, and a faithful old dog. It's the American dream, I suppose " She laughed at this last remark, a somewhat forced laugh.

"What about you?" I asked.

"Me? I work part-time as a nurse in a hospital, and I guess I'm fairly successful—but I work hard. The rest of the time, I simply try to be a good mother and wife."

As she spoke, her voice softened to a near-whisper, and a look of utter sadness swept across her face.

"You seem very close to tears," I ventured.

The moment I said this, Melanie glanced away, her eyes hard and glistening. She appeared to be staring into the distance, her body tense. After several seconds she plucked a tissue from her purse and dabbed embarrassedly, murmuring something about her mascara.

"The truth is, things haven't been going well lately. I'm not sure if it's Mike—my husband—or me or what, but we don't seem to be as close as we used to be. I know he's under a lot of stress at work, but between all the hours he's spending there and the few nights he goes out on the town with his friends—to let off steam, I guess—we just haven't had as much time together as we once had. I try to tell myself that it's all temporary, but sometimes I just get out of hand. I shout at him, I lose my temper with the children, I get lousy . . ."

Her voice trailed off, then found itself again.

"The fact is—and I just don't know why—but I'm beginning to think I'm turning into some kind of bitch. . . ."

A WOMAN WITH A SECRET

As a psychologist, I am used to treating people with all kinds of problems. Sometimes these problems turn out to be relatively simple—two people undergoing change or stress and rubbing each other the wrong way, for example. The issue is basically one of communication and misunderstanding. In Melanie's case, however, I had a notion that something far deeper was wrong.

All my instincts told me that she was extremely concerned about something, but not yet able or willing to talk about it. She was a woman with a secret—a painful one, I sensed—but a woman with pride and a need to appear in control of her feelings. One of the clues was the way her emotions tended to change at lightning speed—sadness one instant, smiles the next. It was as if these emotions were governed by a simple on-off switch. In fact, even after describing herself as a bitch, she seemed to wave the thought away and suddenly perk up again.

"I'm sure it's just a phase we're going through," she said, sitting up, "and I don't know why I'm bothering you with all these silly little problems that I can no doubt handle on my own."

My response to Melanie was immediate. I told her that while she might be a very competent woman, what was troubling her did not seem to be little and certainly not silly, otherwise she would not be as sad as she was. Had she discussed these difficulties with her husband?

She sighed. "I've tried, but there's never a good time. When he comes home he's usually tired and aggravated, and the kids are around—or else he comes home late and by then he's had a few, so there's no real point."

"Does your husband have a drinking problem?" I asked.

"If you mean is he an alcoholic—*no.*" Melanie's voice was momentarily cold with anger.

"I didn't say alcoholic. I asked if you think he drinks too much."

"I don't really know. I guess at times he does, but I know I also tend to overreact."

I asked Melanie what she meant, and she thought for a moment.

"We've had some talks about his drinking—actually, arguments is more like it. But you can't really talk to Mike about booze. He gets very upset."

"Why is that?"

"He says I'm picking on him, that I don't appreciate how rough his job is and all the things he's done for me and the kids. I used to tell him that I didn't mean to pick on him, it was because I loved him and didn't want him to end up like . . ."

"Like who?"

She hesitated for a moment.

"I guess . . . like the way some people end up, the derelicts that you see on the street sometimes."

"I wonder who you were really thinking about," I mused.

Melanie looked at me, a little surprised.

"Do *you* think Mike is an alcoholic?" she asked suddenly.

"It doesn't matter what I think, Melanie. What matters is what you believe. I can't know if he is or isn't, but what I do know is that you are obviously concerned about his drinking. Maybe you can tell me a little more about your concern."

"Well, according to Mike, there is no problem. He says that it's all in my head. Maybe I'm going crazy, I don't know. It's just that Mike was never much of a drinker before, then suddenly things began to change. Now he comes home smelling of booze, and sometimes he's in a good mood and other times he just wants to pick a fight. When I complain, he gets angry, and when I say nothing, he gets just as angry."

GROWING UP WITH FEAR AND SHAME

For the rest of the session I tried to explore other areas of Melanie's life, including her career, her social and personal relationships, and the feelings she had about the world around her. Though she was careful not to say too much about herself, she had already given me an important first glimpse of a rather lonely, frightened person living behind a somewhat false-happy exterior. And though she was prepared to acknowledge that her life was not as she wanted it to be, she seemed also to be apologizing for asking for help.

Our second session was more productive. She appeared more relaxed and more willing to share some of her inner feelings. She seemed to want to talk about her childhood, how she had grown up, the eldest of three (two younger brothers), in what she called a "screwed-up" home. Her father was aggressive and liked to drink, her mother was a very passive person, frail at the best of times, often sick and in bed. The household was a small battleground.

"Dad drank almost every day," she volunteered. "And on weekends he would be especially bad. He'd start to drink in the morning and wouldn't stop until he passed out, then he'd wake up and start all over again."

She added hesitantly, "I guess you could say Dad was an alcoholic."

"You seemed to have difficulty getting that out," I remarked.

"Why shouldn't I?" she shot back. "It isn't easy to admit that your father was a drunk and that he preferred the bottle to his wife and children."

Melanie's lips quivered and her hands trembled as she struggled to contain her emotions. But she was far from done; she seemed determined to go on, to share the deep secrets that she had kept buried for so long. She recalled how often her father would come home drunk and angry.

"No matter what Mom said or did, it would lead to an argument. Usually she would run off to the bedroom crying her eyes out while Dad would go on ranting and raving. Sometimes he would kick the furniture, punch the walls, and threaten to beat us."

"He did actually physically attack Mom several times," she continued. "It didn't happen that often, but when it did it was terrifying. I was always afraid he would kill her or that she might even kill herself. Sometimes I got between them. A couple of times I was going to call the police, but I never did."

Melanie's voice was matter-of-fact, disillusioned.

"Afraid as I was, I guess I was even more ashamed. I didn't want the neighbors or my school friends to find out what was happening, though I realize that almost everyone knew anyway."

Melanie continued, speaking about the frightening ritual of the dinner table—a place where most families commune in happiness, but where her parents would argue furiously.

"It was often so bad that none of us could down our food. Dad used to send my brothers off to the bedroom and strap them later. He never actually hurt me, though—I just wasn't allowed to get up from the table until I'd eaten everything."

"I don't know if I was more afraid or angry—but after finishing the food I'd rush to the bathroom to throw up. Later it reached a point where I'd feel sick even before getting to the table."

Connections and associations had already formed in my mind, but I let Melanie go on. Only a week ago she had claimed to be free of any major problems, had no history to speak of. Suddenly she was filled with memories, and not the kind that qualify for nostalgia. Here there was anger, just a touch of it, and there was hurt: a lot of it.

"I learned at an early age how to calm my parents down. When Dad would come home drunk, even before he and Mom could start arguing, I would distract him."

She explained how she would sit her father down on the sofa in front of the TV, then remove his shoes and fetch his slippers and newspaper and sometimes a cold beer. This would make him smile and he would say how proud he was to have such a terrific little girl.

"When I was ten or eleven I used to get my brothers ready for school," she continued. "Breakfast and lunch, that sort of stuff, because Mom was half the time in bed . . . depressed, I guess."

"It's funny, you know." Melanie smiled fleetingly. "Mom used to tell me stories about her and Dad, how they met and what things were like. It's about the only time I can remember her smiling. She used to say that Dad was a very quiet, handsome man. He was polite and used to treat her like a queen, and he rarely had a drink. She says that Dad changed after the war. When he got back from overseas he had no job and Mom was pregnant, and he started to go through periods of heavy drinking, then he would stop completely. Mom figured that he would gradually settle down, but he didn't, he just got worse. As unhappy as she became, she never left him. I guess deep down, she must have really loved him."

She paused, swallowing hard, tears now beginning to stream weakly down her face. Her makeup started to run, but this time, though she reached for a tissue, she seemed to ignore the problem for a moment, simply staring off into space.

"What are you thinking?" I asked.

"Oh, nothing much . . ."

"Nothing much?" I repeated

"Well, I guess I was just sort of thinking about Mike, the kids, me, nothing in particular."

MASKS AND APPEARANCES

I learned long ago never to put too much faith in appearances. As a therapist working with alcoholics and their families, this is especially important, for alcoholism—the disease of denial, as it is sometimes known—is a condition in which facades are erected at every turn. Alcoholics constantly minimize the true extent of their drinking and deny the harm it is causing, and their spouses and children get drawn into a similarly destructive process as they attempt to mask their feelings of fear, hurt, and shame.

Though there is perhaps a stereotype in our society of the wife of the alcoholic as someone visibly down and out, this is usually *not* the case. The stress of living with a drinker tends to make wives of alcoholics extremely resourceful and resilient. One obvious way they "mask" or compensate, in the initial stages at least, is by keeping up appearances—brave smiles, a "we're-doing-just-fine" attitude, and attractive and neat clothes.

Though I had no way of really knowing at this point whether Melanie was indeed married to an alcoholic, a few signs suggested that possibility. For one thing, though she was not ready to concede that her husband was an alcoholic, Melanie was clearly quite concerned about the extent of his drinking and, as she had put it, Mike's tendency to go "out on the town." For another thing, her attempts to discuss his drinking with him often led to serious arguments. This suggested to me that Mike was quite sensitive about the topic—something one would not usually expect from a casual or social drinker. On the other hand, people who do have a problem with alcohol are usually very defensive and tend to get easily riled when confronted about their drinking. But there was another issue that continued to trouble me.

Melanie and her two brothers had grown up in a characteristically dysfunctional family. Her father was the type of alcoholic who drank daily, was aggressive, often unpredictable, and occasionally violent. Mother had become an ineffectual parent, unable to provide her children with the warmth, love, and emotional support that are so necessary to basic development. Melanie had responded in a way that is typical of many eldest children (particularly daughters). She substituted as part-time mother and even as part-time wife, attempting to fulfill responsibilities beyond her level of maturity, conceivably hoping somehow to put her broken family back together.

There were many questions on my mind. How deeply had Melanie been affected by the horrible experience of her childhood? Was she trying to fix in her marriage what her mother could not fix in her own, or what she as a child was not able to fix? Was she unconsciously trying to prove that she could be a better wife and mother than her own mother had been?

MEETING PRINCE CHARMING

For Melanie, the happiest day of her life was when she met Mike. Even as she spoke about it, a certain girlish fervor flitted across her face and her smile became irrepressible.

She was in high school, eighteen years old, and he was twenty, a junior at college. She was in a bar with two girlfriends when she saw him. He was tall and athletic-looking, somewhat quiet, but clearly sure of himself. To her surprise he offered to buy her a drink, and her heart jumped. Her girlfriends were envious.

Melanie's eyes grew warm at the memory. "It really was sort of like Cinderella and Prince Charming," she said, glowing. "Me, the poor high school girl rescued from this messed-up family, and him the college boy who was all set to go places."

As in the best of storybook romances, they began dating, fell deeply in love, and married about two years later.

Around the same time, Mike graduated in commerce and obtained a promising job in an accounting firm. In the beginning they had many friends, a varied social circle, and an excellent sex life. Melanie wanted to have children almost immediately, but Mike did not. She finally convinced him, however, and two years after marriage gave birth to their first child. Their second boy, unplanned, was born fourteen months later.

It seemed to Melanie that their relationship began to change soon afterward. She was occupied with the children and unable to go out as often; Mike appeared resentful, missing his parties and social life. He began to work longer hours, coming home late at night. On other occasions, he went out with friends, leaving Melanie with the babies.

"At first I didn't mind—I even understood. I was the one who had wanted the children; it hadn't really been his idea. And Mike was so snowed under with expenses—though where the money goes I really don't know—that he felt he had to work more to provide for us. It just seems that we gradually drifted apart."

At times Melanie felt guilty and concerned, at other times she felt angry and bitter. She sensed that Mike was taking her for granted. Even so, after each argument and discussion, things would improve for a while.

During the last two or three years, however, Mike had begun to miss dinner habitually, having supposedly taken on more responsibility at the office. Often when he did get home he would be intoxicated. Melanie sometimes confronted him about this, and he would respond angrily, telling her not to confuse him with her father, the drunk. He knew what he was doing and he certainly wasn't a deadbeat—in fact, maybe if she stopped nagging and pestering him so much, he might "want" to come home earlier.

When I asked Melanie how *she* felt about this, she became uncomfortable. She avoided my gaze, saying she did not know why she had even brought the issue up.

"I agree with Mike that alcohol is not a problem. Sure, he does on occasion get plastered—but who doesn't? It's certainly not serious, and I know he's not an alcoholic."

Despite what she was saying, Melanie's words sounded somehow wooden, unconvincing. When I touched on this, she fell silent for a moment. There was a remoteness in her eyes, and she responded slowly:

"It's just that I've been thinking about it lately—and one of Mike's friends recently joked about his drinking too much. I know he had an impaired-driving charge several months ago—but I don't want to make more out of it than is actually there."

"And what is actually there?" I asked.

It was just a bad phase, Melanie persisted. She had not been sufficiently understanding. Mike was worried about money and providing for the children's college education—and there was lots of pressure at work. He needed to let go sometimes.

"I just wish I could be more mature and not fight with him—maybe if I got a higher-paying job or took better care of my appearance or I don't know what—but things *could* be as they once were. . . ." She sounded plaintive, almost pleading. "It's just a little stormy now, really . . . I'm sure it will blow over and we'll be a family again."

"Melanie," I said softly, "you remind me of that little girl who tried so hard to protect her family and hide her own fear and shame."

I added: "I've been wondering if there may not be some connection between the upset stomach you often had as a child and the cramps and nausea you've been having of late."

Melanie looked at me in disbelief. Suddenly it was as if a small wall had broken, a tiny dam. She began to weep uncontrollably.

APOLOGIES AND ALIENATION

It was a somewhat different-looking Melanie who arrived for the third session. Though dressed smartly, she seemed more casual, more at ease. Gone was the overdone makeup, and my first thought was that "more" of the real Melanie was here—some of the protective shield had been left behind. Or had it?

She began by apologizing for her behavior during the previous visit. When I said I did not understand, she explained:

"You know, causing such a scene, all those childish tears . . ."

Gently, I told Melanie that there was no need to apologize for the pain inside her. Her next response was interesting.

"Yes, but it happened so long ago—I don't want to stay miserable and make my husband and children suffer for what happened to *me* as a child. Mike is a good husband, and I should be making things easier, not harder."

Melanie was pulling what I call a "classic." She was unconsciously separating her past from her present—attributing all her negative feelings to her childhood experiences while denying that her tears were in any way associated with her present situation.

Clearly it was still too frightening for her to make such connections. Her marriage to Mike had been an escape—Mike had rescued her from her messed-up family. How could the nightmare be starting all over again?

In addition to blaming herself for their marital difficulties, Melanie felt that if she assumed more responsibility, if she made herself invaluable, Mike would need and love her more. Was this not just what she had done when she was growing up?

When I observed that Melanie seemed very anxious about not ending up in the same boat she had been in as a child, she did not respond. After a moment, almost shyly, she said: "I get a lot of dreams, some of them recurring and really quite awful. Can I tell you about one I had a few days ago?"

She then told me about the park, the rowboat, and the whirlpool. Though her original version was somewhat convoluted, we gradually simplified it. Slowly, in the course of discussion, she began to make connections, associating her present marriage condition with the sudden appearance of the whirlpool, the overcast sky, her concern for her children and her husband, her paralysis and uncertainty about how to save the situation. Eventually she began to realize that she was no longer sure about her husband's priorities and whether she could count on him to make responsible decisions. When I suggested that she was afraid that her husband was drowning and that he was pulling her and the children down with him, Melanie nodded mutely. When I suggested that the tiny people on the shore might symbolize isolation and alienation, she nodded again.

SAYING NO TO HELP

The next week Melanie telephoned to cancel her session, stating that something had come up, and that she would definitely meet the following week. A few days later, however, she telephoned again, saying that she needed time to think things through by herself. As she put it: "The sessions have been helpful, but this just isn't a good time to continue. I know you probably think I'm crazy and chickening out, but I don't think I am."

I responded that I certainly did not think she was crazy, but that she had a lot of pain inside and I was concerned about her apparent reluctance to deal with it. Nonetheless, the decision had to be hers.

There was a moment of silence, then a terse thank you and goodbye.

Melanie's ambivalence about continuing in therapy is not unusual. She had taken the first few steps toward seeking help, but a part of her was resisting, saying no—things are not that bad, I can handle it. Though many people may be inclined to respond this way initially, wives and children of alcoholics find it particularly difficult to ask for assistance. Many women fear being blamed for their husbands' drinking or they feel inadequate if they cannot get them to stop. Asking for help is like an admission of failure. They feel that it is their duty to take care of their mates and children and to fix whatever domestic problems arise. Children of alcoholics have a similar problem for different reasons. Because of the deprivation experienced in childhood, because of the lack of stability in their home, because of the emotional neglect, because of so many broken promises, they learn not to rely on anyone except themselves. They find it very difficult to trust others, especially with their feelings, because they have been let down and hurt too many times. They survive by adjusting, and they take a great deal of pride in their strength and self-sufficiency. Surrendering their pride, admitting to needing help, results in a feeling of vulnerability, the dropping of a defense mechanism that has protected them throughout most of their lives. Melanie was the daughter of an alcoholic father, and possibly the wife of an alcoholic man. I sensed that she would have to work her way through these twin issues. Would she find her way out? Would she and her husband resolve the situation on their own? Would she perhaps return for therapy?

I had a feeling I might hear from her again. But for the time being, these were questions I would have to live with.

WIVES: SOMETHING IN COMMON

Going through this book, as you read the various case histories and reactions, you may—if you are or have been involved with an alcoholic—come to recognize certain traits and key situations that have attended your relationship.

No two alcoholics necessarily behave in the same way or suffer quite the same consequences from their drinking. Similarly, no two women are affected by a husband's alcoholism in quite the same way. One woman may become deeply depressed and avoid social situations; another may find new outside interests and activities which create a life completely separate from that of her husband.

Even with such differences, however, there are certain characteristics and patterns of behavior that are fairly common among wives of alcoholics. Some women *cover up* for the alcoholic (as with a telephone call to the boss, saying the husband is sick, when in reality he is too drunk to work); others *take over* his abandoned responsibilities (pay the bills, negotiate with creditors); and still others *blame themselves* for the problems created by his alcoholism (like Melanie: "If I got a higher-paying job or took better care of my appearance or I don't know what . . .").

By engaging in the above actions, they are attempting to control and minimize the potentially horrid consequences of their mate's alcoholism. The objective is personal and family survival. Unfortunately, the price a wife pays is often tragically high. Part of that price includes gradual alienation and isolation from others.

Mixed with all of this confusion, not surprisingly, is a variety of turbulent emotions—guilt, anger, fear, anxiety, and shame, to name only a few. I will take a broader look at the role of these emotions when the time comes.

WIVES: SOMETHING UNCOMMON

Though these are fairly typical, normal human reactions to problems in living, if left unattended they can become serious, chronic patterns of behavior affecting all aspects of an individual's perception and attitudes toward herself and the world around her. Wives of alcoholics need attention, understanding, and emotional support.

Most of all they need to know that they have alternatives. Historically they have received very little of this kind of help. On the other hand, their instincts to survive by doing whatever is necessary to protect themselves and their family have been interpreted by many professionals as evidence of intent to keep the alcoholic drinking and symptomatic of their own "illness." In a certain sense this has become as much a tragedy as the experience of living with an alcoholic. Some professionals treat her as a villain, others treat her as a sick, disturbed victim, and still others treat her as almost incidental to the issue of alcoholism. But very few treat her as a human being.

The major focus of attention for clinicians and researchers, until the last decade, was the alcoholic male, while wives and children and other family members were somewhat ignored. This was partly due to a belief—a myth, even—that if the alcoholic recovered the family would also recover.

This is far from true. A woman's problems do not necessarily diminish when her alcoholic husband stops drinking. Often they persist under different guises, for her feelings and attitudes have been deeply affected, leaving—for anyone who truly cares to look— long-lasting scars. Unless dealt with, these afflictions can undermine whatever attempts at recovery are made, by *all* concerned—husband, and wife, and children.

Key Points

• Women who live with alcoholics are survivors. They do whatever is necessary to protect themselves and their families from the potential consequences of their mates' abusive drinking.

• Support is essential. Whether your alcoholic mate stops drinking or not, your personal problems *can* be addressed and resolved. If your recovery acts as a catalyst for your mate's recovery, so much the better—but one should not be contingent upon the other.

• Despite what you may think, and what others may tell you, chances are the feelings you have are not the least bit "abnormal." What you have been through, no matter what the temptations are to ignore it, should *not* be pushed aside or minimized.

• You are not alone. There is help—and, as we intend to make clear, there is hope.

Voices: *Various women*

WHAT ATTRACTED ME . . .

• **Louise:** "I knew from the very beginning that he drank too much. But I also knew that he had been hurt a lot. He had been orphaned in childhood and later lost his brother in Vietnam. When we met at night school, he was going through a very painful divorce. It seemed he had a lot of reasons to drink. Naïvely, though, I thought all he needed was love. If he found the right woman and settled down, he'd no longer need to drink, or at least not as much. In my mind, I was that woman. I would cure him with my love and we'd live happily ever after. I couldn't, of course. It took Alcoholics Anonymous to get him unhooked. Thanks to them, I now hope we truly can live happily ever after."

• **Marjorie:** "During the early days of our relationship, his drinking didn't seem so bad. Though he almost always had a few drinks inside him, he was fun to be with. Sometimes he would be tender and considerate, other times wildly imaginative and full of jokes. Ironically, the alcohol seemed to bring out the best in him—in the beginning, that is .   "

• **Veronica:** "Let me put it this way: What kind of man turns up at your door at one in the morning with flowers in his hand? Then tells you that he has wine and cheese in a taxi waiting downstairs, that he wants to take you up to the lake for a firelight picnic? He was not like other men I had met. In the beginning his unpredictability was exciting—later there was no excitement, just unpredictability."

• **Yvonne:** "The man I met was an unpublished poet, and for some reason it seemed to me that writers are notorious for drinking. I loved the way he spoke and the way he thought. In the beginning he wrote many poems to me, and I was flattered. I was quite awed by his talent, impressed by the loveliness he seemed able to pull out of his heart and turn into words. He told me that booze freed him up—he called it "American passion"—and I thought maybe the trade-off was a good one, drinking for art's sake, so to speak. After a couple of years I changed my mind. The poems got repetitive, and so did the drinking. I don't believe he ever did get published."

• **Martine:** "He was a warm, honest, emotionally open human being. We became great friends before we were lovers, and when we married, I thought I must be the luckiest woman in the world. For many years I continued to feel that way, although life certainly wasn't always smooth. It wasn't until the children had grown up and Stan was facing retirement that our problems began. First it was pills, then it was booze. Pills for energy and pills to relax and pills to sleep and finally beer to swallow the pills. I thought he was going through a phase. Some phase—it drove us apart and almost cost him his life. He's in a drug-and-alcohol treatment center now and I hope one day to feel again like the luckiest woman in the world."

• **Grace:** "I was a drinker myself, back in those days. We were both university students, sowing what I guess are called 'wild oats.' We would drink wine on campus, get plastered at the local hangout, party till the small hours at one frat house or another. Drinking became a form of communication between us, a lot of ups and downs, a lot of craziness, but a lot of fun also. I enjoyed his company, and the fact that he was a drinking buddy just seemed to add to the attraction. After we graduated we continued living together, but things got a bit more serious—jobs and responsibility, career and ambition, that sort of thing. I instinctively cut back on my drinking, without any problem, since I guess I'm not alcoholic. Unfortunately, he couldn't do the same. He just seemed to get worse and worse, and eventually we split. I still think about him though, still care for him. . . ."

• **Jackie:** "I fell in love with Gary because I found him exciting. He liked fast cars, was great in bed, could party all night, and could drink everybody under the table. But that was then. Now he doesn't drive a car because he lost his license for drunk driving. He has little interest in sex, he has hardly anyone to party with, and he drinks *himself* under the table."

• **Bonnie:** "What can I say? When I met Bob, I thought he was divine. He was well-mannered, affluent, intelligent, and sensitive. He took me to the best restaurants and all the top shows. When I wasn't well, he cared for me like nobody had ever done before. But eventually it all began to come apart. In the end, I lost my darling Bobby and in the process almost lost myself too. No, I didn't lose Bobby to another woman—I lost him to a bottle."

• **Ronda:** "I fell in love with Donald because he represented everything I valued. He was honest, faithful, and dependable. When he made a commitment to anybody, he always followed through. Over the years, though, as his drinking increased, alcohol gradually took control of him, and in the end it robbed him of everything he valued, including his dignity, honor, and self-respect. Even more, it robbed me and the kids of the man we loved."

Two

Victims or Villains?

A normal woman would not tolerate such a situation;
these women need the role and so suffer it. . . .

—M. L. Gaertner, *The Alcoholic Marriage* (1939)

Are women who develop relationships with alcoholics *different* from other women? Are they victims of circumstance, or the authors of their own destiny? Are they simply unfortunates who happen to have strayed into a web called alcoholism, or do they deliberately seek out an alcoholic mate in hope of satisfying certain deep-rooted needs within themselves? Does such a woman really want her mate to stop drinking, or does she only say so? Does she support his efforts to stop, or does she unconsciously impede his progress and undermine his attempts?

By now you might well be asking yourself, what kind of questions are these? They are surely not serious. If anything, they seem designed to give offense. Any woman who has ever been through the turmoil and terror of living with an alcoholic, whose hopes, dreams, and family life have been shattered by the bottle, could scarcely be blamed—in the face of such remarks—for feeling stunned, angry, and hopelessly misunderstood.

On the other hand, the question does exist: *Is* it just possible that such women—including those who have died at the hands of an alcoholic partner or who have chosen to take their own lives as a desperate, final solution to their anguish—deliberately committed themselves to a relationship with a man they knew to be alcoholic or susceptible to alcoholism? Is it remotely possible that these women avoid seeking help and stay in such relationships because they are disturbed people? Is it conceivable that they derive some "sick" satisfaction from such a relationship?

Let us look at some of the things that have been said in this area.

HOW WIVES HAVE BEEN SEEN

Historically, two major psychological perspectives have dominated our understanding of wives of alcoholics and influenced societal attitudes toward them. One describes these women as villains while the other sees them as victims. What is noteworthy, however, is that even when perceived as a victim, the wife continues to be blamed in one way or another for her own suffering as well as for that of her children and alcoholic mate.

In addition to the foregoing, a third perspective has also been emerging in recent years, one which tends to describe wives' behavior as symptomatic of illness. Many professionals no longer consider alcoholism to be a disease associated with just the drinker, they view it as a *family* disease—all who live with the alcoholic are said to become as sick as, or sicker than, the drinker. This so-called family disease has variously been referred to as coaddiction, coalcoholism, or codependency.

Once the disease manifests, codependents are said to behave in a manner that is not in their own best interest and that unintentionally supports and prolongs the drinking of the alcoholic. In short, this is just another way of saying that wives are somehow to blame for their own suffering as well as for the suffering of those around them.

In simplest terms, then, it does not appear to matter which psychological perspective one draws from. Whether victim, villain, or "diseased," wives of alcoholics are somehow seen as responsible, directly or indirectly, for the difficulties incurred by alcoholism.

THE WIFE AS VILLAIN

In the Bible, in Genesis 3:11, God confronts Adam and Eve:

> "Have you eaten of the tree of which I commanded you not to eat?"
> The man said, "The woman whom thou gavest to be with me, she
> gave me fruit of the tree, and I ate." Then the Lord God said to the
> woman, "What is this that you have done?"

To some extent this is what happens to wives of alcoholics. The man
may taste the forbidden fruit—in this case, alcohol—but the woman
is called to account. Indeed, it is one of the truly unfortunate and
tragic aspects of alcoholism that women who have endured so much
hardship as a result of a partner's drinking have also been blamed for
the problem. Wives of alcoholics have been accused:

- of purposely choosing an alcoholic as a mate or husband, or of
  purposely choosing a man with a personality susceptible to alcoholism.
- of doing nothing to encourage the mate to stop drinking (if he
  already had a problem) or of causing or contributing to the
  development of his drinking problem if he was not initially
  alcoholic.
- of impeding or blocking the alcoholic's efforts to stop drinking.
- of attempting to sabotage the alcoholic's sobriety after he stops
  drinking.
- of falling apart emotionally if the alcoholic succeeds in remaining
  abstinent.

THE WIFE AS DISTURBED PERSONALITY

The foregoing assumptions—or accusations, as I have called them—
form the framework of what is known as the Disturbed Personality
Hypothesis, or DPH. Although this theory, originally popular around
the 1940s and 1950s, has gradually waned, it continues to affect the
way in which wives of alcoholics are perceived even to this day. On
the other hand, it also represents one of the first attempts by
professionals to focus attention on the predicament of these women;
before that, spouses and children of alcoholics were largely neglected.

According to proponents of this hypothesis, women who marry alcoholics do so because they themselves are deeply disturbed individuals who were raised in very dysfunctional families. As a result, such women grow into adulthood suffering from anxiety, hostility, insecurity, sexual inadequacy, and masochism. Their interpersonal relationships, especially with men, become marked by a strong need for control, related to mistrust of others, and by fear of rejection.

These women consequently become attracted to alcoholic or prealcoholic men because such men are often thought to be weak, needy, dependent, and easily dominated. Marriage or any other form of committed relationship to an alcoholic or potentially alcoholic male is thus an unconscious effort on the woman's part to resolve or at least mask her own inadequacies and to satisfy her severely neurotic underlying needs.

GETTING SATISFACTION THROUGH MISERY

How can a normal woman gain satisfaction from a relationship with an alcoholic mate? Quite simply, she cannot. But these women are not considered normal to begin with, which changes everything. As we have seen, supporters of the Disturbed Personality Hypothesis describe wives of alcoholics as masochistic, hostile, sexually inadequate, and overly controlling. A relationship with an alcoholic, however, offers such women a measure of appeasement. How does it do that?

- *Masochism:* As the drinker's dependency on alcohol increases, he becomes less able to interact with others. Responsibility, communication, and intimacy are all affected, and the wife is often left feeling rejected, unwanted, unloved, and unnecessary. She may be repeatedly embarrassed and humiliated by the drinker's behavior, or even physically abused, and though a so-called normal woman would not put up with this, the masochist's need to gain pleasure from pain is obviously satisfied. According to Gaertner,* the female psychotherapist quoted at the beginning of this chapter, while a

*Gaertner, M. L. *The Alcoholic Marriage*. Thesis, New York School of Social Work, 1939.

wife of an alcoholic may complain about her suffering, these complaints are superficial. In the end she stays with her mate because she is able to feel like a martyr and needs to suffer.

- *Hostility:* Alcoholics are notoriously unreliable, their lives frequently characterized by broken promises, forgotten engagements, missed appointments, and unpredictable or obnoxious, drunken behavior. Clearly such a person makes an obvious target for criticism. His wife uses these shortcomings as justification for venting her stored aggression. She can scream and yell and even throw things with considerable impunity. Though her rage is a product of her own past, she is able to pretend that he is the cause.

- *Frigidity:* In a similar way, an alcoholic's drinking provides an excellent opportunity for a wife to resolve or mask her supposed sexual inadequacy. Alcoholism may decrease the drinker's sexual desire or limit his performance, which suits his frigid wife perfectly. On the other hand, if his sexual desire and ability remain unaffected, his wife can use the drinking as an excuse to punish her husband by denying him sex. Either way, she can have sex less often and not feel guilty, since she has placed all the blame on the alcoholic. As Margaret Lewis, another psychotherapist, wrote: "Their anxiety about their own sexuality might have been part of the reason for the attraction to weak men."*

- *Control:* Since alcoholism often results in neglect of responsibilities and obligations inside and outside the home, a wife is often "forced" to take over these abandoned roles. This gives her more authority in the relationship and makes her husband all the more dependent on her. Eventually she achieves her basic need, to gain control.

In addition to the foregoing, clinicians pointed to the fact that many of these women were unwilling to cooperate in getting their husbands to stop drinking. They either would not attend therapy or, if they did, would talk about the past and express considerable anger even though the mate was making an effort to conquer his addiction. This was seen as an attempt to sabotage his treatment and further confirmation of how disturbed wives of alcoholics really are.

As well, it was noted that numerous women did not appear to feel any better or happier even after their mate *had* stopped drinking.

*Lewis, M. L. The Initial Contact with Wives of Alcoholics. *Social Casework*, 1954, 35, 8–14.

Some actually appeared to do worse, complaining about psychosomatic ailments such as headaches, backaches, and gastrointestinal pains. Some developed sleep disorders and various psychiatric symptoms that were not present when their mates were still imbibing.

Taken together, all of the above points add up to a picture of the wife as villain, while the husband emerges as the somewhat innocent victim. Gaertner, (previously cited), expresses this fact clearly when she writes: ". . . if the caseworker can help the wife release some of the pent-up hostility aimed at the husband, he will be spared at least a little of the nagging and ridicule which emphasize his inadequacy as the head of the family and are part of the pattern driving him to drink."*

It is difficult to say if this is the origin of the notion of "driving him to drink," but it is certainly one of the more formal renditions of it.

FLAWS IN THE VILLAIN CONCEPT

Though there are many other equally plausible and rational ways of explaining the behavior of wives of alcoholics, ways that are not insulting, accusatory, or suggestive of sickness, these appear to have been ignored by supporters of the Disturbed Personality Hypothesis. As we will see more clearly in the next chapter, there are numerous reasons why a woman may stay with an alcoholic mate that have nothing to do with disturbance, and everything to do with lack of choice.

When one considers the period in which the Disturbed Personality Hypothesis was popular, it is actually somewhat surprising that so many female mental-health professionals were at the forefront of these accusations—being women, they would surely have been aware of the social constraints placed upon women of their day. After all, this was a time when divorce was greatly frowned upon, when single mothers were shunned, when day care did not exist, when women did not generally have careers to turn to for financial survival, and when treatment for alcoholism was not readily available. Yet in spite of all these obstacles to walking out of a marriage, the decision to remain with an alcoholic was viewed as masochism.

A similar paradox surrounds the issue of hostility. If the stress of

*Gaertner, 1939, p. 43.

living with habitual drunkenness causes a wife to feel frustrated and bitter, and she expresses these emotions by screaming, arguing, pleading, and crying—is this not *normal* behavior? Indeed, when she appears to be in control of her emotions and there is no overt anger over her husband's drinking, specialists have been inclined to interpret this as a sign of withdrawal or depression or denial, or even as a lack of concern for her husband's well-being. Once more, the wife appears to have been placed in a no-win situation.

The notion of sexual inadequacy can also be seen in a thoroughly different light. Why, for example, would anyone want to have sex with someone who habitually stinks of stale beer, or who has thrown up in bed on previous occasions, or whose drunken behavior and attitude are repugnant? Why would any woman acquiesce to having sexual relations with a partner who does not seem to give a damn about her outside the bedroom? Refusing to have sex under such conditions, I believe, is not symptomatic of sexual inadequacy, but a sign of sexual maturity and healthy assertiveness.

Let us think, too, about the question of control. When a wife takes over the budget, pays the rent, and assumes other responsibilities that her husband has systematically neglected, she is said to be compensating for feelings of insecurity and mistrust by being overly authoritative. If the same woman, however, refused to let her children climb into the car with her husband when he had been drinking—or if she herself insisted on driving—would that constitute an overly controlling wife? Clearly not. She would be trying to protect her children, herself, and maybe her alcoholic mate too; she would be trying to ensure the survival of her family in the face of a difficult and out-of-control problem.

The observation that many women do not appear to be overjoyed or overly enthusiastic when their mate finally goes on the wagon or that some women even appear despondent and withdrawn was used to support the premise that they prefer him drinking. On the other hand, is it not just as reasonable to conclude that a wife may break down when her husband ceases drinking—that she is at last able to allow herself to *feel* once again? She has been struggling so hard just to meet the basics, just to survive, that she has simply not been able to give much attention to her own emotional distress. Now, indeed, is the time she should be helped, not blamed. She is not sabotaging his abstinence, she is coming out of her own personal hell, and she feels scared, bitter, and neglected.

THE QUESTION OF SUSCEPTIBILITY

There is a further problem with the Disturbed Personality Hypothesis. Researchers long ago determined that many alcoholics were either not drinking at all—or certainly not to excess—when they married, indicating that their wives had not chosen an alcoholic mate. In response to this, supporters of the Disturbed Personality Hypothesis simply suggested that these women chose men whose personalities were susceptible to alcoholism.

It is illogical to make statements about women being attracted to men who are prealcoholic unless it can first be proved that there is a way to predict alcoholism in an individual. Scientific investigation has not been able to identify a personality unique to all alcoholics, and efforts to predict alcoholism have been thoroughly unsuccessful. How on earth, then, were these women, thoroughly unskilled and untrained in the field of alcoholism, able to identify men who had a predisposition toward becoming alcoholic?

Alcoholism is considered a disease whose cause continues to be hotly debated but presently remains elusive. Even so, according to supporters of the hypothesis, wives of alcoholics are able to induce this disease and possibly make it worse if it is already present. Ridiculous as it may seen, this is almost akin to suggesting that they are carriers of an unknown virus or bacteria.

VARIABILITY AMONG WIVES

While the idea of wives somehow "infecting" their mates with alcoholism clearly strains credulity, it is nonetheless probable that some wives of alcoholics are indeed psychiatrically disturbed, and that they were so prior to the onset of their husband's alcoholism. Certainly there are people who are mentally and emotionally unstable, and it would be only reasonable to assume that some of these may be women who end up married to alcoholics.

But to make sweeping generalizations about an entire group of people based solely on the fact that they are married to an alcoholic man simply does not make sense. Wives of alcoholics are not a homogeneous population; they differ from each other according to such obvious factors as age, religion, culture, upbringing, education, life experience, and ability to cope with stress. They have, in short, neither identical personalities nor identical attitudes.

In addition, the circumstances and environment in which the drama of their lives is played out may be very different. Some have children while others do not. The children may be infants or they may be older or they may already have left home. Some women are financially well-off in spite of the alcoholism while others are in dire poverty because of it. Some may have support systems consisting of family and friends while others may be orphaned and friendless with no support system whatsoever. What is more, their mates—the alcoholics themselves—differ from one another in numerous ways, including type of drinker, style of drinking, and severity of consequences, and this again adds to the complexity.

It is difficult to imagine that any group of individuals who differ from each other in so many ways could possibly be affected and react to one common variable—marriage to an alcoholic—in exactly the same manner. There must be hundreds, maybe even thousands, possibly even millions, of different "types" of wives of alcoholics.

FOUR TYPES OF WIVES

It is interesting to note that one proponent of the Disturbed Personality Hypothesis, Thelma Whalen, actually did try to differentiate among wives of alcoholics, classifying them into four separate groups:

- "Suffering Susan," whose need to punish herself leads her to marry an alcoholic, who will provide her with the misery she requires.
- "Controlling Catherine," whose unconscious distrust of men leads her to marry a weak alcoholic whom she can control.
- "Wavering Winifred," who unconsciously defends against her low self-esteem by marrying an inadequate man so that she will feel needed and important, despite ambivalence, or wavering, about the price she must pay to satisfy this need.
- "Punitive Polly," usually a professional woman, who must compete with, defeat, and punish men, and thus often chooses an alcoholic for this purpose.*

Although Whalen's report is somewhat typical of the simplistic and consistently negative view held by proponents of the Disturbed

*Whalen, T. "Wives of Alcoholics: Four Types Observed in a Family Service Agency." *Quarterly Journal of Studies on Alcoholics*, 1953, 14, 632–641.

Personality Hypothesis, it is nonetheless significant in that it represents one of the first and, to this day, one of the rare attempts to draw attention to the notion of variability among wives of alcoholics.

As we will eventually see, this concept—the idea of differences among wives—is extremely important, both from a professional standpoint and from the standpoint of wives themselves.

THE IMPACT ON TODAY

It has been suggested that the Disturbed Personality Hypothesis is merely a reflection of the attitudes and values of the period in which it was conceived, that it is reflective of a male-dominated society in which women are often scapegoats. Though one could probably make a good argument for this, it would only detract from the real complexity of the issue.

The alcoholic marriage, its effects on the nonalcoholic wife, her responses to it, and the theories about these women cannot be understood in terms of any single explanation. Many factors have contributed to the present situation, not the least of which is our overall limited knowledge about alcoholism and its effect on those who live with alcoholics. Another major factor is that professionals have for a long time held very negative attitudes toward alcoholics (and continue to do so); by extension they have also shown negativity toward their spouses and children.

Of much greater concern, however, is that the Disturbed Personality Hypothesis has continued to shape and influence the way therapists perceive wives of alcoholics to this very day. It has stigmatized such women, created false negative stereotypes, and further contributed to their already low self-esteem. What is more, it has affected the ways in which intervention is applied and has impeded the development of more creative, appropriate, and adequate services for these individuals. In short, what the alcoholic and his alcoholism failed to accomplish, this well-intentioned hypothesis succeeded in doing.

Today's theories about wives of alcoholics and the alcoholic marriage are not much different from those of a few decades ago; they are merely better disguised and expressed in more seductive and subtle language, including a number of questionable labels. To gain a clearer picture of this, however, we should first look at an alternative theory—one that characterizes wives as victims—and see how this has gradually given way to the concept of codependency, the notion that wives are "sick."

WIVES AS VICTIMS

It was not until the mid-1950s that professional opinion about wives of alcoholics began to shift away from the Disturbed Personality Hypothesis. Based mainly on the clinical work and research findings of Joan Jackson, new ideas and formulations began to evolve, and the Sociological Stress Theory, or SST, was born.

According to supporters of the Stress Theory, wives of alcoholics are not villains, but rather victims of an alcoholic spouse. These women do not have deeply disturbed personalities that lead them to marry an alcoholic or so-called prealcoholic man, they do not cause their mates' drinking problem, and they do not take pleasure in the pain and suffering that is part of such a relationship. On the other hand, whatever emotional or behavioral difficulties these women have, though considered to be a result of the stress and strain of living with an alcoholic, are nevertheless viewed as psychopathological. The stress and strain of living with an active alcoholic results in psychological disturbance, and the wife's efforts to adjust and cope with her mate's behavior result in "enabling" him to continue drinking.

Many supporters of the Stress Theory believed that wives of alcoholics go through identical stages of adjustment and coping. These stages can be loosely divided into three phases—early, middle, and final.

- *Early Phase:* Wives of alcoholics rationalize their mate's behavior and deny that there is a problem. They cover up, lie for him, and make excuses for him. Without intending to, they "enable" him to continue drinking.
- *Middle Phase:* The wife argues, begs, and pleads with the alcoholic to stop drinking. She attempts to control his behavior by refusing to have sexual relations, refusing to socialize with him, and may even threaten to leave. She may try to hide his bottles, break them, or pour them out. Many women continue to deny that there is a problem and also continue to defend and protect their mate from outside criticism. This of course "enables" the alcoholic to continue

drinking. He is so angry about his wife's negative attitude and behavior that he may drink even more.

• *Late Phase:* As the situation deteriorates, the wife is no longer able to deny that there is a problem. She stops arguing and fighting, and may even emotionally detach herself from her mate. She takes over responsibilities that he has neglected or abandoned. Since her husband now does not have to worry about obligations and commitments, she has unintentionally further enabled him to go on drinking. In addition, her emotional detachment and coldness leave him feeling bitter and unloved and he has therefore even more of an excuse to go on drinking.

Though supporters of the Stress Theory do not see wives of alcoholics as disturbed women who purposely seek out a relationship with an alcoholic, they nevertheless see them as psychologically disturbed because of the stress of living with an active alcoholic. The Stress Theory does not support the view that wives of alcoholics deny their mate's alcoholism because they want or need him to drink. Nor does it attribute her anger (breaking bottles, threatening to leave, quarreling, and so forth) to innate hostility and aggression. Nor, for that matter, does it view her taking over responsibilities as evidence of a need to dominate and control. It does, however, view all of this behavior as *enabling* the alcoholic to drink.

In brief, then, though wives of alcoholics are not initially disturbed, they become so as a result of living with an alcoholic. And though they do *not* intentionally seek to marry an alcoholic, they unintentionally provoke or enable him to go on drinking. No, the wife is not a villain, she is a victim—but somehow she is as much a victim of her own making as she is of his drinking.

In contemporary terms, the idea of enabling has been aided and abetted by such labels as "coalcoholic," "near-alcoholic," "coaddict," and "codependent." While alcoholism is seen as the disease of the drinker, codependency is being promoted as the disease of those who live with him. The upshot is that wives are thus considered sick and in need of treatment

LABELS THAT DISABLE

When we describe someone as coalcoholic, what exactly are we saying? To my mind the implication is that the person spoken about is somehow an accessory or accomplice to the alcoholic and all the wrongdoing that his drinking may entail. A similar case might be made for the terms "coaddict" and "codependent." Likewise, what about the word "enabler?" When applied to an unpleasant reality—such as alcoholism is—the expression takes on an equally unpleasant connotation. It is as though we were speaking about a person who "enables" a crime to take place by averting his or her gaze.

Wives of alcoholics are consistently tagged with the above labels. Not only this, they are also accused of denial, lying, covering up, protecting, excusing, and defending their mates' behavior. The fact is, the terms used to describe the behavior of these women are at best negative, at worst somewhat synonymous with the language used to describe deviant or irresponsible behavior.

The point is simple. Words influence—they can enhance or distort the way we perceive reality. When we affix negative labels to wives of alcoholics, these women start to look negative, feel negative, and suffer negative treatment at the hands of society and professionals, who should know better.

The majority of professionals who employ these labels will insist—and legitimately—that they do not blame women for causing their mates' alcoholism. Nonetheless, the words exert their own hidden effect. Living with an alcoholic is itself a very painful ordeal. What makes it even more difficult is that the alcoholic tends to deny his drinking problem and to project blame onto everyone and everything other than the bottle and himself, the most common target being, of course, the wife.

Because many people, including wives of alcoholics, are either uninformed or misinformed about alcoholism, they fail to understand the denial of the alcoholic. They thus tend to feed neatly into his itinerary of excuses and explanations. Also, since in many of his accusations there is a hint of truth, the wife is often inveigled into accepting at least some if not a great deal of the blame for his behavior. This contributes not only to feelings of guilt and shame but also to a gradual loss of self-esteem and self-confidence.

The irony of the whole situation—and it is a tragic one—is that many therapists are inclined to interpret these feelings and consequent coping styles as illness, as we have already seen. They then attach their negative labels to describe the disturbance, and inadvertently succeed in adding to the low self-esteem and low self-confidence that these women already have and that they, the therapists, initially set out to cure. In some sort of unintentional but convoluted way, they end up supporting the alcoholic's accusations that his drinking is related to his wife's disturbance or sickness.

WIVES AS "SICK"

One of the most questionable terms of all those applied to wives of alcoholics is "codependency." The expression started to become popular around the 1970s, and although its origins are somewhat obscure, the concept itself is all too familiar. It is just a new word used to dress an old idea—to camouflage and perpetuate the notion that wives of alcoholics are sick people badly in need of psychotherapy.

I will not attempt to give an exact meaning for "codependency," simply because there is no single agreed-upon psychological definition of it. In fact, to stretch a point, it might almost be said that there are about as many interpretations of the word as there are professionals using it. Some describe it as a learned behavioral problem; others say that it is a personality disorder; still others say it is something that *resembles* a personality disorder; and many others say that it is a disease.

According to some theorists, codependency is caused by living with or loving an alcoholic, who may be one's spouse, parent, grandparent, or close friend. Other theorists see the cause as involvement with anyone who is chemically dependent, and still others regard codependency as an innate part of an individual's makeup that responds to involvement with an alcoholic. To add to the potpourri, there are some specialists who claim that codependency may have nothing to do with alcohol or other chemicals but is the result of growing up in any type of disturbed family environment.

The characteristics and behavior of the individual who is supposedly afflicted with this condition are so general and all-inclusive that one wonders if there is anyone left on this planet who is *not* codependent. Codependents deny that they are involved with an alcoholic or that they have personal problems; they attempt to control others; they are confused and cannot express their real feelings; they feel depressed, angry, afraid, worried, and anxious; they have low self-esteem and low self-confidence, and they often develop stress-related medical complications.

One could go on and on describing the characteristics of codependents, but it would probably consume a good portion of this chapter—and there is really no point to it. Though there is no single definition and both the causes and characteristics vary considerably, the concept has been employed almost exclusively in connection with wives of alcoholics. Furthermore, the way these women are affected and the way they respond to or attempt to cope with a mate's excessive drinking is described as the *disease* of codependency.

There is so much wrong factually and morally with this concept that one scarcely knows where to begin to attack it. Describing women who are living with or married to an alcoholic as codependent suggests that these women are all the same—sharing the same experiences and consequences—and we know that is absolutely not true. Even when the effects are similar, wives tend to perceive and interpret the problem differently, and they also attempt to cope with the situation in a multitude of ways that can be very different from one woman to another. Perhaps this explains the numerous definitions and characteristics needed to describe codependents—so that no woman who is involved with an alcoholic will feel forgotten or left out.

A second problem with the term "codependency" is the link it establishes. Just because an alcoholic is considered to be dependent on alcohol does not make the spouse or lover *co*alcoholic, *co*addicted, *co*dependent, or *co*-anything. Why should she not be just who she is and be given the dignity and respect of retaining her own individuality and identity? If her mate were mentally deficient would she be codeficient? If he developed a disease such as epilepsy or diabetes would she be a coepileptic or codiabetic? Is it not enough that a woman married to an alcoholic share the agony and grief of his disease? Must we also make her share the disease in name?

CODEPENDENCY AND SICKNESS

Wives of alcoholics are emotionally affected in numerous ways—but are they really sick? The answer is almost unequivocally no. In feeling the way she does and in attempting to cope in the way she does, the wife shows signs of health, not sickness. It is natural and healthy to feel bitter about a man who is destroying one's life and one's family.

It is also understandable that a wife feels worried and even pities her mate, because this is a man she certainly once loved a great deal and perhaps still does. If alcoholism were considered to be willful misconduct, then we might legitimately ask ourselves how she can feel pity for such a man. But if we say that alcoholism is an illness, then it makes little sense to criticize the woman who loves him for being concerned about what is happening to her sick husband. It is as if certain professionals are looking for any way in which to interpret the wife's behavior as illness.

We speak about emotional and mental disturbance when an individual does not behave in a manner appropriate to a given circumstance. Here we have an entire population of women who are behaving in a manner most appropriate to their circumstances, and their actions are defined as indicative of disturbance and a need for psychiatry. Why?

Part of the answer is that we are living in a sickness-oriented rather than a health-oriented society. In other words, by virtue of our training and diagnostic ability, we are often so busy looking for the telltale flaw, the hidden hint of sickness, that we fail to recognize signs of health. In short, for health we can do nothing, so we look for sickness, because we have remedies for that.

Many people who are quite normal suffer from problems in living, and wives of alcoholics suffer from a very specific problem—they are living with an alcoholic. There is no question that the experience may bring on a wide range of negative emotions. But this is surely a most appropriate reaction to a very painful and frightening problem in life. How, therefore, does this translate into codependence and thus sickness?

According to at least one author, codependence is a disease because it has a clearly identifiable onset (the point at which the individual's life is not working), it has a definable course (the continued deterioration of the individual, emotionally and mentally), and if it is not treated, there is a predictable outcome (death).

If this is the basis for determining that so-called codependency is a disease, then almost anything in life is a disease—in fact, life itself is a disease. It has a clear onset (birth) and a definable course (the human being after initially growing and developing begins to deteriorate physically and mentally), and whether it is treated or not, the outcome is predictable—in fact, guaranteed. It is death.

The logic of such arguments defies comprehension.

ALTERNATIVES

The time is well overdue to stop accusing wives of alcoholics for everything and anything they do or fail to do. The name-calling should stop—they are *not* codependent, coalcoholic, coaddicted, near-alcoholic, or enablers, they are just human beings living in a tremendously difficult situation that requires immediate, urgent attention. They need proper information, education, and support. They need professional services that will treat them in an understanding, sensitive manner and help highlight how well they have actually done in their efforts to keep themselves and their families bonded together against spectacular odds.

Tragically, this is unlikely to happen. There are those who will not be satisfied until they have "pathologized" the behavior of these women—in other words, until they have identified their behavior as a form of disease. There is even a suggestion that codependency not only be retained as an appropriate term, but be adopted into the official psychiatric handbook, *Diagnostic and Statistical Manual of Mental Disorders*, as a legitimate personality disorder. I, for one, hope that this idea will be carefully reconsidered. The additional harm that this would do to wives of alcoholics is unconscionable.

"Codependency," just like its predecessors "coalcoholic" and "coaddiction" and its contemporary "enabler," is an absolutely unsatisfactory and insidious term. Granting it further status as a disease only adds to the damage already done by the alcoholic and his bottle.

Similarly, when attempts to cope are defined as enabling, the responsibility for drinking or not drinking is turned over to the wife. My understanding has always been that alcoholics do not need to be enabled to drink. They are quite adept at enabling themselves whatever the circumstances, if that is what they choose to do.

The alcoholic needs to assume responsibility for his disease and for doing something about it. Instead, well-intentioned theorists too often pass the buck and point the finger at the wife. Where the wife needs understanding, she receives negative labels. The unfortunate result is that all too often she is condemned even before she enters the specialist's office.

Key Points

• If you are living with an alcoholic, you are in a relationship with someone who is sick, whose disease is alcoholism. He will not get better until he stops drinking. Though certainly affected by it, you yourself are *not* diseased.

• Some of the ways you have coped have helped you survive, but you cannot do it alone. Some of the ways you have coped have not helped;

you need information about alcoholism. You need to know what is available in terms of support.

• You are a survivor—but even survivors pay a price and have limits. There is no shame in reaching out for help and support.

Voices: *Tina, a wife*

"THE TOUGHEST THING I EVER DID"

I lived with Pablo for almost five years. When I first met him he swept me off my feet as no other man had done before—and, for that matter, as no other man has done since. He was charming, witty, well dressed, and well mannered, and he had a good job as a journalist. It was clear from the outset that he liked to drink, but he quickly rationalized this, describing himself as a *bon vivant*. Needless to say, I accepted this without a shred of concern; it seemed such an integral part of his character. And I admit there was something novel and exciting about being in the company of a man-about-town. We always seemed to be on the go, always partying, clubbing, going to upscale restaurants or little out-of-the-way places that I would never have found in a million years. In just a matter of weeks I met more people—bar types, as a rule—than one would believe possible.

Perhaps the thing I liked most about Pablo, the thing that most attracted me, was his tremendous youthfulness, his zest for life. He was a few years older than I, in his early thirties, but he frankly looked ten years younger. And his philosophy, his attitude, seemed to reflect this. Once, jokingly, I asked him what was the "secret" of this eternal boyishness. He merely smiled and picked up his glass. "Good living," he said, nodding toward his drink. There was, I thought, a touch of self-mockery in his voice as he said this, a touch of irony. And then he added, "I guess my entire body has been preserved by this stuff."

I don't believe I thought much about his response at the time; I probably found it mildly humorous. Now, of course, I can read something into it. In the same vein, I didn't think too much about his apartment at the time, though I was kind of surprised by the state of it. For a person who dressed so well, who exuded so much verve and worldliness, his place was a terrible mess. The garbage was full of empty bottles and containers of take-out food. There was an inch of dust on the furniture. The bed was unmade. The refrigerator was bare.

Pablo was clearly someone who had difficulty coping with day-to-day living—but again, I accepted his explanation: He had been through a rather difficult breakup with a girlfriend—she had recently moved out—and since then he had somehow never really managed to get motivated about doing housework. Under the circumstances, and knowing Pablo, I saw a certain plausibility to all this. I felt sorry for him. Dumb as it seems in retrospect, I immediately set about cleaning up. While I was doing this, Pablo set off for the restaurant to buy supper for us. He returned three hours later, two bottles of wine under his arm and a large pizza in his hands—he had run into an old friend, had had a couple of drinks, and had failed to notice the time. He was extremely apologetic. And, typically, he offered me a flower, a way of saying sorry. He had plucked the flower from someone's garden.

Perhaps, as in the Beatles song, I should have known better. But the fact is, I didn't. I loved Pablo, I thought he needed help to get his life back on track, and I thought I was the person to provide that help. I thought that his constant drinking was a reaction to his recent breakup. I thought I could be a sort of Joan of Arc for him, someone who would rescue him from the regular bouts of despair that seemed to plague him. Frankly, this kind of thinking resulted in one of the biggest mistakes in my life.

After a few months we began to live together, Pablo with me. In the beginning I was in ecstasy. Every evening was an occasion for romance, for candlelight and wine. Lovemaking was great, and so too was conversation. Pablo was a very sensitive man, and at times his words made me feel like the most important, the most beautiful woman in the world. But gradually things began to change. I began to notice flaws. I noticed that our suppers began to consist of more wine and less candlelight. My belief that Pablo's drinking was a reaction to the breakup began to waver. Then Pablo lost his job.

On and off, I supported him for almost four years. During that time, despite certain doubts, I continued naively with the notion that I was Pablo's savior. What I had taken to be boyishness suddenly acquired new meaning. I began to see Pablo as being as helpless as a child, unable to stand on his own feet. Without me, what would become of him? The thought worried me no end. That he did virtually nothing around the apartment was a given. Though I worked full-time and paid the rent, I was also the one who cleaned up, who provided food, who did the laundry, who bought—and picked out—clothes for Pablo. I seemed always to be treating him to something or other. Though I tried to refrain from giving him money to drink, I even broke down on this level from time to time. It seemed, more and more, that sympathy was replacing passion. It seemed, more and more, that instead of a man I had a child on my hands.

One evening, quite by accident, I ran into Pablo's former girlfriend at a party. Once the connection was made, we ended up talking about the one thing we had in common—this man-child we both knew intimately. I had had a few drinks myself (I had begun to drink somewhat liberally at that point) and I found myself opening up rather drastically, somewhat bitterly. After listening to my veiled complaints for several minutes, the ex-girlfriend suddenly gazed at me quizzically. "Don't you know what Pablo *is?*" she asked quietly. I was not sure what she meant, but she was quick to fill in the answer. "Pablo is an alcoholic," she said. "Why do you think *I* left?"

If someone had told me there was a death in the family, I don't think I could have been more crushed or horrified. Yet somehow I felt taunted by the ex-girlfriend's remark, challenged by it. I started asking around, finding out what I could about alcoholism. I even got myself into Al-Anon. I read a book about codependency, and the idea rather frightened me. The fact is, I didn't *want* to be a mother-figure for Pablo. While it might have appeared to give me pleasure, I can honestly say it didn't. I can say equally honestly that what I felt for Pablo was certainly love, and legitimate human concern—not to mention a certain amount of doubt about how to proceed.

The toughest thing I ever did was to kick Pablo out. I was breaking inside. Pablo might be alcoholic, but he was not a bad man—and he had a wealth of qualities, even in the heart of his drinking. Maybe he was too sensitive for the world, I don't know. Nor do I know why God created such goodness and such torment side by side in the same human soul. I spent a lot of sleepless nights thinking about this.

Even so, when all was said and done, I laid everything on the line with Pablo, told him that while I cared for him, he would have to do something about his drinking. I could not guarantee that I would wait for him, I could guarantee nothing.

Pablo left, hurt and drunk. I had to close my mind to this fact. And I did not hear from him for a month or so. I did not know if he was drunk, falling in love with another woman, or—worse still—had become depressed to the point of suicide. Then one evening there was a phone call.

The man I met half an hour later was very different from the man I had come to know. His eyes were clear, he was well-dressed, and he was sober. He spoke with pleasant but restrained humor. He had joined AA. He had just made a series of applications for work and was to be interviewed the following day. He had in his hand, interestingly, a pink rose, store-bought.

It took months before Pablo and I got back together. It took longer before I was truly able to trust him again. But it all did happen, and today we have a child and are deeply in love. Today I am a mother in the proper sense. Today I am "codependent" in a way that satisfies *me* perfectly. I depend on my husband and child for love and support. They depend on me for love and support. None of us, thank God, is dependent on any bottle, or anything that comes out of it.

Three

Alcohostages

every prison that men build
Is built with bricks of shame.

—Oscar Wilde, *The Ballad of Reading Gaol*

His drinking had not always been a problem. True, Bob had enjoyed his booze—in retrospect, maybe a little too much—but it had never resulted in any serious problems and there had never seemed any real reason for concern. Sure, there were those odd occasions when he had clearly had too much, but even then it was mostly good fun and certainly nothing to be alarmed about.

When, Carla wondered, had it all gotten out of hand? Had there been a specific day or week or month when everything suddenly changed? Or had it been a gradual process? What had caused it? Was it her fault? Had she not shown him enough love? Or should she have been able to see what was happening, and could she have done something about it?

It all seemed to Carla like a bad dream as she sat outside the emergency room awaiting news from the doctor. It seemed like days since she had received the telephone call informing her that Bob had been involved in a serious traffic accident. It had in fact been only a matter of hours. The details still hadn't sunk in: something about two fatalities, about Bob being intoxicated and running a red light.

The years of their relationship flooded through her mind. There had

60

once been so much love and caring. So many dreams they had shared: the new home, Bob's thriving career, the three lovely children they had had together. Suddenly, as Carla reflected, the feelings of guilt and sadness clustered into anger and then into rage—how could he have done this to them? How could she have let him?

His drinking had really gotten out of hand the last two or three years. Many a night she had sat up worrying about whether he would make it home safely. When he would finally arrive she would feel bitter and foolish for having been anxious for nothing. She had told Bob time and again how worried she was about his drinking, how she felt like a prisoner, locked into a situation she was powerless over. She had tried to reason with him, but he had simply assured her that he was in control and that she should lay off. During the last few months they had had some terrible arguments about his drinking and neglect of her and the children, and finally she had moved out.

Now, only hours after arguing with him on the telephone, her worst nightmare had come true. Two strangers were dead, and her husband was fighting for his life. Had she been right in refusing his plea to move back together? If she had said yes, would the accident have occurred? And if she had moved back, would anything have changed?

Tearfully, silently, alone in the deserted waiting room, she wondered if she would ever truly know the answer. She wondered,too, if it was all going to end tonight—or had it really all ended long ago?

WHY WOMEN STAY

For anyone who has never been involved with an alcoholic, the fact that many women stay in such relationships must be somewhat puzzling. They are adults, after all, with freedom of choice. There are social services, self-help groups, an entire battery of apparent solutions. Why then do they continue on in a situation that is unfulfilling, unrewarding, hurtful, or humiliating? They do so for three principle reasons:

- They have little or no alternative; they are trapped.
- Though there are reasonable options, they are either unable to see them or they fear taking a chance—they are stuck.
- Though there are reasonable options and they are aware of them

and able to conceive of employing them, they choose to stay for numerous rational reasons of their own.

Findings have indicated that as many as nine out of ten women married to alcoholics and with children under age eighteen remain married, while only one out of ten men married to alcoholic women under similar circumstances stays. This phenomenon perplexed and intrigued investigators, and they attempted to find out why it was so, with the result that most of their eventual explanations turned out to be somewhat negative. Some experts, as we have seen, suggested that such women remain because they are masochistic, or because they need to control their relationships with others and feel they can easily dominate an alcoholic mate. Other experts suggested that such women suffer from the caretaker syndrome—a need to take care of others even to one's own detriment—and that the alcoholic provides an excellent opportunity to do just that.

Unfortunately, none of the foregoing explanations attempts to consider the possibility that there is a host of equally plausible—and *positive*—reasons why a woman might stay with her alcoholic mate.

- She may simply have accepted that no relationship is perfect, and that one does not bail out at the first sign of trouble.
- She may have decided that she should, temporarily at least, put his needs ahead of her own.
- She may have decided that the consequences of her husband's excessive drinking are not severe enough to warrant separation or divorce. If he is not violent and not verbally abusive, if he keeps the family financially secure, if his general behavior is not humiliating to the family and his drunkenness is far from being a daily occurrence, then she may feel that she is better off keeping the family together rather than facing the uncertainty and upheaval of terminating the marriage.
- She may not yet have recognized the partner's drinking as alcoholism. She may believe that his drinking problem is merely a temporary phase he is going through, and is therefore prepared to give her mate the benefit of the doubt.
- She may have chosen to stay because she recognizes alcoholism as a disease and feels it her responsibility to help the person she loves get better—or, at least, not worse—just as she would if he had any

other disease. She may be fearful that leaving him will result in his further deterioration, and even death.

• She may not even have begun to exhaust different ways of coping or getting him to change, and until she does she cannot be sure that she may not in fact be able to get her mate to stop drinking.

• She may have chosen to stay for religious, moral, or cultural reasons. She may have married at a time when separation and divorce were considered virtually taboo, when the attitude was to marry for better or worse. She may continue to stay because of the stigma or sin associated with separation or divorce; or she may see termination of the marriage as a reflection of her failure as a woman.

• She may have chosen to stay because of guilt and self-blame. Her husband may have accused her of being demanding, nagging, lacking understanding and support—as alcoholics often do. She may feel that there is some truth to what he says and may try to rectify the situation. Many women convince themselves that they are responsible or to blame for the situation. By doing so they are able to maintain a sense of hope that if they themselves make adjustments he too will change.

OTHER REASONS FOR STAYING

Fear, too, is sometimes at the root of a wife's decision to stay with her husband. If one has not lived with a violent, abusive partner, it is very difficult to grasp the true enormity of such fear, the manner in which it slowly paralyzes. But not all alcoholics, of course, are violent—there are other reasons for staying:

Many women simply have no support system—neither family nor friends who are able or willing to aid and shelter them. Living in a state of friendlessness, being cut off from family, often goes hand in hand with marriage to an active alcoholic.

For women with youngsters, the problem may be lack of money. Children need shelter, food, clothing, medical care, and education. If the children are young, the mother may need to be with them and may thus be unable to work and support herself. Even if she could find responsible trained help, much of her pay would probably be spent on baby-sitting costs.

If small children are not the issue, it may be that a wife has never worked and has no employable skills, or that she worked many years ago and is now at an age where finding employment is very difficult. Coupled with the lack of self-confidence that often characterizes wives of alcoholics, the task of finding a job may seem insurmountable.

Another problem is that not all women have the information and knowledge or sophistication necessary to make use of the various community services available to help them. For other women the issue may be that they live in remote areas where appropriate help and services may not be available, or at least not easily accessible.

These are just a few examples—but there are countless other reasons why a woman might choose to stay. And, right or wrong, these reasons have nothing to do with being sick, disturbed, coalcoholic, codependent, or an enabler. Though a therapist would be wise to review carefully a woman's motives for staying, it is not his or her domain to judge and label her decision as an indication of sickness or weakness just because he or she sees the solution differently. There is, to my mind, a much more profound issue behind the decision.

WIVES AS HOSTAGES

Not all prisons have bars or walls or guards standing watch in towers. Likewise, not all hostages are taken by force or held at gunpoint. Many are held captive by circumstance, by their own beliefs and values, even by love. Wives of alcoholics are just such hostages—held captive by an emotional involvement with a fugitive from reality and responsibility.

What happens to these women is not unlike what happens to hostages taken under other conditions: Unable to mollify their captors, they attempt to adjust to the situation as best they can, the object being to survive. Rather than referring to them as enablers or any of the other dubious and negative terms we have examined, I see these women as "alcohostages": hostages of an alcoholic and his disease.

Most of these women did not enter into a relationship with an alcoholic; they fell in love with a man—a man they thought they could share their hopes, dreams, and life with. That the man eventually became addicted to a mood-altering substance was neither their fault, their wish, nor their choice. It was simply a matter of human misfortune, for both partners. Even in instances where women do marry a man who may already be drinking alcoholically, they do so with the unfortunate belief that the condition is temporary or at least not serious. Let's not forget too that love is indeed often blind, and it is easy to overlook or minimize the shortcomings of someone we care about.

Whatever their reasons for continuing on in the relationship, these women are stuck—trapped in a no-win situation. What they need is help, support, and understanding. What they receive, instead, is criticism, blame, and judgment.

OBSERVATIONS ABOUT HOSTAGES

The taking of hostages has become an all too familiar occurrence in today's world, and although our understanding of the psychological consequences of such captivity is still slight, much has been learned during the last few years. It is apparent that victims of a hostage-taking are often not only deeply affected at the time, but continue to experience a wide range of problems weeks, months, and even years after having been freed.

It is worth noting, nonetheless, that not all victims are affected in the same way or to the same extent. The question of whether such differences are related to length of captivity, severity of confinement, or to the innate characteristics, personality, and coping style of the victim remains unanswered. In all likelihood, however, each of these variables plays a role in how a victim is affected. Yet in spite of differences, observers have identified a number of patterns among victims. For instance, while in captivity:

- Victims experience a profound sense of helplessness and powerlessness; they see no way out.
- Victims experience humiliation, often feeling debased as a result of their lack of control over what is happening.
- Victims often tend to be dependent on their captors for almost all their needs, and thus become much like children; they are forced to seek permission for almost everything they do, including going to the bathroom.
- Victims often begin to feel dehumanized, valueless, and insignificant.
- Victims frequently feel bewildered and confused, not understanding what is happening to them or why.
- Victims attempt to cope with their situation by adjusting as best they can, the sole purpose being to survive.

A further effect is that some victims bond with their captor—a phenomenon popularly referred to as the Stockholm Syndrome. (The name comes from an incident in the Swedish capital in which bank robbers held several customers hostage; when police burst in, a captive tried to protect one of the criminals. There have been similar reported incidents in which hostages have even fallen in love with their captors or have maintained relationships after the ordeal was over.)

The Stockholm Syndrome is generally believed to be a defensive function whereby the hostage unconsciously tries to reduce his or her anxiety, fear, and helplessness. The victim forges an emotional bond with the captor to feel safer; the victim believes that it is potentially more difficult for the captor to harm someone he or she cares about.

SIMILARITIES BETWEEN HOSTAGES AND ALCOHOSTAGES

Women married to alcoholics often tend to be as much hostages as any individual who is held captive against his or her will. Many act and react in ways similar to other hostages and are affected by the experience of living with an alcoholic in much the way that hostages of terrorist kidnappings are affected. Though an alcohostage may not have an actual gun to her head, the issue of leaving, of escaping, is often no less difficult and unrealistic. In some ways it may be even harder.

While the terrorist is driven by an ideology for which he is ready to sacrifice his life, the alcoholic is driven by an equally powerful dependency on a drug for which he is prepared to sacrifice almost everything, including his life (one need only look at the statistics). Just as the terrorist and his victim are strangers and the terrorist presumably has little or no compunction about killing his captive, the alcoholic can become a transformed personality who under the influence is capable of the most irresponsible behavior, including violence. Just as the hostage sees no escape, the alcohostage also sees no way out, no viable alternative or option.

The alcohostage, like the hostage, feels an overwhelming sense of helplessness and powerlessness. No matter what she does or tries, she soon discovers that she has no control over the alcoholic's drinking. She experiences shame and humiliation as a result both of the drinking itself and of her inability to control it. As happens to other hostages, her self-worth, self-esteem, and confidence are deeply shaken. The alcohostage is left feeling confused and bewildered, unable to comprehend fully what is happening around her and to her and what to do about it.

Just as the hostage has nobody to turn to and either sees no escape or fears to chance it, so too the alcohostage feels that there is nobody to turn to, nobody who can understand or help. Just as the hostage may dream of release or rescue while fearing that any attempt at rescue could result in tragedy, so too the alcohostage lives with a hope and a dream that the misery will end, but a fear that the intervention of therapists or others might make matters worse.

Both the hostage and the alcohostage feel isolated and alienated from friends and relatives. While the hostage has been forcibly separated from them, the alcohostage finds friends drifting away— or she herself weaves her own isolation out of shame. Both the hostage and the alcohostage are overcome with feelings of anxiety, fear, and panic as well as feelings of anger, outrage, and hatred. While some hostages may develop feelings of sympathy and understanding for their captor's cause, many alcohostages feel pity and worry for their alcoholic captor. Frustrated, frightened, and cut off from the world they used to know, hostages and alcohostages attempt to cope by adjusting and by doing whatever is necessary to survive.

Yet, in spite of all, one captive draws our sympathy while the other draws our scorn. While the victims of a terrorist are called hostages, the victims of an abusive drinker are called enablers. While one is seen as courageous, the other is seen as codependent. When a hostage develops a bond with a captor, who just hours or days earlier was a stranger, it is viewed as a defense mechanism; but when an alcohostage continues to love the man she married, but who now is alcoholic, her behavior is seen as a symptom of family disease, emotional disturbance, or personality disorder.

AFTER THE HOSTAGE ORDEAL

Even after they have been freed, many victims of a terrorist hostage-taking continue to experience emotional and psychological problems. They do not automatically or immediately pick up the fragments of their lives and return to their previous level of functioning. They continue to live with memories and fears.

Seamen aboard the *Pueblo*, the U.S. Navy vessel seized by North

Korean gunboats in 1968, were held hostage for nearly a year. According to many of these men, the experience created a painful and lasting effect. Although some were eventually able to adjust and get on with their lives in reasonable fashion, others continued to be deeply affected even years later.

Researchers have found that many hostages continue to experience feelings of anxiety and tension for a considerable time after their captivity is over. Some develop phobias and suffer from sleep disturbance; others experience sharp mood swings, have vague physical complaints, and feel alienated and misunderstood. Even after these symptoms dissipate, the ordeal is often reexperienced through nightmares and memories. These flashbacks can be precipitated by a chance remark or action, or by a certain sound or scene.

Some hostages have explained that the sudden realization of being free can itself be frightening and bewildering and takes time to get used to. A good example of this occurs in the comments of Anatoly Shcharansky, the Jewish human rights activist who spent years in Soviet prisons, isolated from his loved ones. In his autobiography, *Fear No Evil*, he writes that when he suddenly realized he was about to be set free, his dominant emotion was sorrow—not joy. He felt overwhelmed by fear of freedom and a sense of having no self-confidence. Later, after being reunited with his family, he experienced difficulties sleeping, for sleep took him back "to the black-and-white world of the Gulag."

According to Dr. Martin Symonds, a psychiatrist at the New York University School of Medicine, victims can experience what he calls a "second injury" if they perceive rejection or a lack of expected support after their victimization. Some victims apparently feel ashamed of how they conducted themselves while in captivity and tend to blame themselves or others for their unfortunate experience. He suggests that at least some of this shame may be related to positive feelings that were developed toward the captor. He also emphasizes the importance of continually reassuring victims of terror that their behavior during captivity is understandable and acceptable—that the main issue is that they were able to survive.

AFTER THE ALCOHOSTAGE ORDEAL

When we look at wives of alcoholics we see a pattern similar to that of hostages after their release. If a mate succeeds in stopping drinking, or if a wife has succeeded in freeing herself from the relationship, she is not automatically overjoyed and ready to get on with her life. Many such women continue to behave with caution and mistrust, and some appear even more depressed than before.

Observations of this kind, as we have seen, led various experts to conclude that these women prefer their mates to keep drinking and maybe even need to suffer. If this is so, how many of us would make the same inference about hostages of terrorists—would conclude that their difficulty in readjusting, their continued depression and anger, indicate that they actually prefer being held hostage, that they need to suffer and are obviously sick people? None of us, I believe, would draw this conclusion. Why, then, are wives of alcoholics not perceived with the same kind of fair-mindedness? Why are their courageous efforts to cope and adjust and protect their children seen as a sickness?

There are U.S., British, and other citizens being held hostage today in the Middle East, and I hope they will be home long before this book is published. But how will we receive them? If they do not appear to be as overjoyed and excited to see us as we are to see them, will we conclude that they preferred to remain where they were? If they appear sad, depressed, and distant, will we conclude that they are mentally disturbed, that they have some other form of illness or personality disorder? Of course not. We will understand that they have been through an ordeal, that they have lived in hell. We will try to be supportive and understanding.

Why, then, do we not treat our hostages at home this way? When will we begin to show that kind of compassion, sympathy, and understanding for wives of alcoholics—the alcohostages—instead of mislabeling them and accusing them of mental instability?

ADVANTAGES OF THE HOSTAGE PARADIGM

Comparing wives of alcoholics to hostages is an effort to reflect their predicament more accurately and realistically while, at the same time, neither stigmatizing nor judging them. "Hostage" is a neutral term, a statement of fact akin to saying: "He is a man, she is a woman, that is a building." It is not a medical or psychiatric diagnosis, and it does not presume anything about the individual's health, personality, behavior, attitudes, or values. The term "alcohostage" describes a particular type of hostage—an individual who is either emotionally or physically trapped in a relationship with an alcoholic. (Although the word is being used in the context of wives of alcoholics, it may just as easily refer to husbands and children of alcoholics.)

There are certain advantages in describing and thinking about wives as alcohostages. Aside from being neither insulting nor prejudicial, the term does not presume that a wife is sick or emotionally disturbed or has a personality disorder. It leaves the door open, so that each individual can be understood in her own right, rather than as a negative stereotype. It gives women an opportunity to seek help without feeling that there is something psychiatrically wrong with them or that they are somehow at fault for their own victimization.

It is a fact that hostages and other victims of crime and terrorism are generally unwilling to seek therapy in the first place. Some feel ashamed, others feel they may be partly to blame for their own misfortune, and still others feel that psychiatric treatment is itself adding insult to injury. Labeling wives with negative terms is not only insulting, it further alienates them from the very people who might be able to help them.

ONE MORE PRISONER

I met Carla for the first time in the early winter of 1984, barely five months after that long, anguished night in the hospital waiting room. Bob, as it turned out, did die. He never regained consciousness and succumbed that same night during surgery.

Carla had never recovered from the tragedy. Her grief had turned to self-hatred, and though she had not been much of a drinker, just taking an occasional glass of wine, her drinking was now clearly out of control and self-destructive. Not only this, she was also relying heavily on sleeping pills.

She had made the appointment at the insistence of her parents and older brother, who had become concerned about her behavior and inability to take care of the children. The children were living temporarily with their grandparents, while Carla obtained whatever help she needed.

The Carla I met at that first appointment was a very sad and lonely person, but even more, she seemed like a person burdened by the weight of insurmountable pain. Although potentially an attractive woman—she was in her mid-thirties, slim and dark-haired with high cheekbones—the ravages of sorrow and drink had stolen much of the expression from her face. Her gaze was somewhat stony, her voice, her words, faintly impersonal.

The preliminaries did not last very long. Carla wanted to talk, needed to unload, and once she started there was no stopping. First she spoke about her thoughts and feelings the night of Bob's accident. Then she touched on many issues—her children, her marriage, Bob's death, her drinking, her parents—but there was one common theme throughout. It was regret. Regret about her failure as daughter, mother, and wife. Regret about the argument she had had with Bob just before the accident. Regret about his death and for not having done enough to help him with his drinking problem. But most of all there was the regret—and the guilt—that she had not had the opportunity to apologize to Bob before his death, that she had not been able to tell him how much she really did love him in spite of his drinking and her quarrels with him.

There was another point. Though Carla had finally summoned the strength to leave, she had for many years been much like the alcohostages I have described. And even after she left, the tie was still there, the doubt about whether or not she had made the right decision. With Bob's death, this ambivalence had not ebbed; it had merely grown stronger, to the point of seeming unbearable.

"I just don't know if I can live with myself anymore," she said tearfully. "I just don't know if what I did was right, or even okay. I felt so trapped when I was in the marriage—and now I feel even more trapped, as though I'm in a prison, as though I've been given a lifetime sentence. Did I ever really have a choice? Did I ever really have *any* choice?"

Much of the time, Carla appeared to be talking only to herself, her emotional pain so severe that she seemed oblivious to the fact that there was anyone else in the room.

Key Points

• Feeling trapped in an alcoholic marriage is not unusual. Doing something about the feeling, and the reality, is essential.

• Many women in alcoholic marriages exhibit traits similar to those shown by hostages. Like hostages, they attempt to cope by adjusting and by doing whatever is necessary to survive. Though there is a tendency to feel shame about this, it is important to credit oneself for being a survivor—for having displayed courage under very difficult circumstances.

• Emerging from a hostagelike situation, you may continue to be affected long after. You need understanding and support, possibly from a professional source. Though you may be wary of accepting help, it is available and desirable.

Voices: Stephanie

LOOKING BACK IN ANGER

Jeff and I met at a friend's party during my senior year at college. He was several years older than me, and though he didn't look my type, he was certainly not an unattractive man. We danced a bit, talked a lot, and before the evening was over, he asked me for a date.

We went out the following week and I really enjoyed myself. Jeff was a gentleman. I still remember how he pulled the chair out for me at the restaurant table and, later in the evening, when I excused myself to go to the washroom, Jeff stood up—as he did when I returned. I don't know why I was so impressed by these seemingly little things, maybe because most guys just wouldn't bother, but it made me feel very special.

We went out several more times and then I spent the night at his place. Like everything else with Jeff, sex was great, but not for the usual reasons. It was the way he touched me, the softness of his hands, the calm voice and the warmth I felt when he put his arms around me. In time we got to know each other very well. Jeff was a highly successful photographer, owned his own studio, lived in a beautiful apartment, had expensive taste, enjoyed fine dining and good conversation. Though he was single, he had once been engaged but it hadn't worked out.

We continued to spend a lot of time together, and most nights I stayed at his place. I began bringing more clothes over there, mainly for convenience, I told myself. Though I wasn't living with Jeff, I unofficially moved in without officially moving out of my dormitory residence. But within a few months it was official.

On the first anniversary of our living together, Jeff took me out for a special evening on the town. We went back to the restaurant where we had had our first date. During dinner, Jeff presented me with a gorgeous diamond ring and asked me to be his wife. I was so happy I couldn't stop crying. People must have thought that something terrible had happened, but it was the most wonderful moment of my life. Jeff ordered a bottle of fine wine, then another and another. I hardly drank, partly because I was too excited and partly because I wasn't much of a drinker. It was then that I suddenly remembered what Jeff had told me long ago. He said that he had given up booze because he once "almost" had a serious problem with it. Though he never spoke very much about this so-called problem with alcohol, it dawned on me that this was the first time I had ever seen him drink. I wasn't so much shocked as curious, and I remarked to him, "I thought you said that you don't drink alcohol?" He responded immediately, "I don't, but this is a very special occasion, and besides, since when is wine considered alcohol?" He was right. It *was* a very special occasion, and though I let it go at that, I felt a little uneasy.

We got married, and a month later I found out I was pregnant. When I told Jeff, I just couldn't believe his excitement. He actually had tears in his eyes. But the following months became the beginning of the most difficult part of my life. Though I didn't doubt for a moment that Jeff loved me and wanted the child, his behavior was changing quite dramatically. His moods became unpredictable. He would be calm and serene one moment and angry and shouting the next moment. He'd make arrangements with me and cancel at the last minute, or he just wouldn't show up without even informing me.

I also began to receive calls from his clients, who sounded very irate. There were complaints about jobs that had not been done properly, and about missed appointments and improper billings. When I'd give Jeff the messages, he'd start shouting and blaming everybody else, but it was never his fault. I don't know why it took me so long to make the connection between Jeff's drinking and his behavior, but when I finally did, it was too late. When I told him about my concern, he denied that there was any problem. When I persisted, he told me to go to hell, that I was an immature little dictator and no different than Brenda. Who was Brenda? It turned out that Brenda was the woman he had onced been engaged to.

The picture was becoming clearer. I began to realize that what had happened to Jeff and Brenda was now happening to us, and I didn't know what to do, who to turn to. When Brenda left Jeff, she was nineteen, she wasn't married, she wasn't pregnant, and she had a job. I was twenty-eight, married, expecting a child, and suffering regular bouts of morning sickness. In addition, I had given up my career to be a mother and wife. I felt scared and trapped. My dreams were coming apart and I had no control over what was happening. It became painfully clear that if things were to work out, Jeff would have to get help, but that wasn't about to happen. Though I considered the various options available to me, none seemed to be realistic. I was virtually living in a prison.

I stayed with Jeff for nearly two more years, and in the end left him, taking the baby with me. Although life was difficult at times, it was heaven compared to how life had become with my "gentleman."

Four

Is He or Isn't He?

The vast literature on alcoholism is with few exceptions
an apology for not being able to do much about it.

—Eric Berne, M.D.

Carla's story, as she outlined it to me, was of truly tragic proportions.
She had been confronted by a terrible quandary. Though she had
cared for her husband deeply, she recognized that he was slowly
poisoning himself with alcohol. Not only that, he was also poisoning
the well-being of the entire family—turning love into bitterness, trust
into distrust, and security into fear. Carla was affected, the children
were affected, every fiber of domestic life was affected. What, then,
was she to do? Should she put aside her love and leave her husband
to his fate? Or should she sacrifice herself and the children by staying,
by maintaining her marital vows and trying to help a man who
seemed incapable of being helped?

Having been raised in a family in which there was scarcely any
drinking, Carla was unfamiliar with alcoholism. To her, it was one of
those rare conditions that happened to people who were unemployed,
uneducated, homeless—certainly not to people like herself or her
husband. Though she had never particularly cared for Bob's drinking,
she had reluctantly accepted it as something men enjoy doing on
occasion, like watching a Sunday-afternoon football game.

When she first noticed that Bob's pattern of drinking had changed, in both quantity and regularity, she became quite alarmed. Discussions led to arguments, and arguments led to blaming and counter-blaming and threats of separation. These skirmishes were followed by apologies and promises and short-lived periods of less drinking or total abstinence, but the cycle repeated itself time and again. When Carla began finding bottles stashed around the house, however—in the basement, in the toolshed, and in various closets—she sensed that the problem was well beyond her control. Even so, leaving Bob was too hard to face. As an alternative, she decided to seek the advice of a counselor.

During months of therapy sessions, Carla learned a great deal about alcoholism and especially how it affects the family. She began to recognize the patterns and the crazy merry-go-round she was on. Gradually she learned to let go, to detach: no more arguments, quarrels, or threats. Leaving Bob was still something she was not ready to face, but not letting his drinking run her life was one thing she did have control over. She made a point of not worrying about whether he would be home for dinner or not, and she enrolled in evening adult education courses.

Then one afternoon Bob's boss telephoned to ask if there was something wrong. He said that Bob no longer seemed to be himself, and that he was missing a lot of time at work. Though Carla sorely wanted to talk openly, to ask the boss for advice on how to help her husband, she found herself parroting Bob's own explanation—that he was going through a stressful period. She embellished the excuse further, saying that Bob had not been well, but that he was being looked after, and would soon be back to his old self. After the call, Carla felt dirty. She also felt very angry that she had somehow been put into a position of covering up for her husband. What on earth was happening to her?

When she brought the incident up at her next therapy session, the counselor asked why she had lied to Bob's boss. Carla explained that it was almost instinctive. The last thing in the world she and the children needed was for Bob to lose his job—who would pay the mortgage, who would pay for the children's education? The counselor pointed out to Carla that she was enabling her husband to continue drinking, that because of her lying and covering up Bob was able to continue doing as he pleased. After weighing this information carefully, Carla decided that enough was enough. Maybe if she took the three boys and lived with her parents, Bob would finally realize that he needed to go for help.

With the support of her therapist, Carla finally made her move, and Bob was devastated. His drinking increased radically. Often, late at night, he would call her, rambling into the telephone about how much he missed her. Other times he would harangue her about how she had abandoned him in time of need. Carla was heartbroken, confused, and filled with conflict, but she maintained her position: Bob would have to do something about his drinking before she would consider returning.

During one late-night call, Bob, though clearly intoxicated, finally indicated that if Carla and the children came home, he would give up all drinking and would also go for therapy. Carla stood fast, telling him to fix the problem first, then she would make a decision—she had heard Bob make such commitments too many times before. Despite the firmness of her statement, Bob continued to badger her, his tone becoming wilder and more irate. Carla could finally take no more, and hung up.

It was after this call that Bob ran a red light in a drunken stupor. And it was a while after his untimely death that Carla came to see me, bottled up with questions about whether she should have said yes to Bob that night, whether she should have hung up, whether she should ever have left in the first place.

As I watched this poor woman struggling with grief and regret, I was overcome with sadness. But there was another emotion, too. It was frustration, the awareness that Carla had been impeccably correct in her assertion that alcoholism is such a "mysterious and frightening" thing. At that moment, I could think of no two adjectives that summed up the disease more accurately.

A DISEASE WITHOUT DEFINITION

A colleague who was confronted by a particularly difficult case once remarked to me, borrowing from Mark Twain, "Alcoholism is a bit like bad weather. Everyone talks about it, but no one seems to do anything about it."

Her feelings were quite understandable. In proportion to all the discussion surrounding alcoholism, the number of real scientific breakthroughs appears small indeed. This is not to say that we do not now know a great deal more about this complex disorder than we used to; we do. But we still know far too little—and certainly less than we pretend to.

Though a wealth of information has been gathered on the subject—as early as 1942 it was suggested that perhaps as many as 100,000 books and papers had addressed the topic—there is still no single clear and fully agreed-upon definition of alcoholism, of exactly what it is and what causes it. Even experts who have devoted a lifetime to the study of this baffling condition find themselves in regular disagreement about it.

THE PROBLEM OF DOUBT

If experts cannot agree, is it any wonder that wives have difficulty determining whether a partner is alcoholic? So often, the issue for a wife, in the early stages of recognition, at least, is not one of denial—though it may appear that way—but one of legitimate doubt. What, for example, are the differences between a heavy drinker, a problem drinker, and an alcoholic? (Some experts insist there are subtle but significant distinctions.) How does one know if a husband's drinking, though excessive and regular, is not actually temporary? How does one know if a husband, rather than being alcoholic, is not simply drinking in response to a specific run of circumstance?

The fact is, one often *cannot* tell—and this is the unhappy inability that frequently befalls the wife of an alcoholic. She is, in a sense, required to make a judgment call in a realm where exceptions tend to be the rule. And in a society that attaches enormous shame to the word "alcoholic," who in her right mind would want to take the chance of mistakenly branding another human being—especially a spouse, a loved one—with such a stigma?

Other aspects, of course, feed into the wife's dilemma. One is that most alcoholics, by virtue of their addiction, can find no end of marvelously "logical" reasons to justify why they drink; alcoholics tend to be remarkably persuasive and convincing.

Another is that the wife is subject to what some psychologists call "reflected" stigma. In other words, if a wife *knows* that she is living with an active alcoholic, what does it say about her? Does it make her a bad or weak person? Does it make her—as discussed in Chapter 2—a contributor or accomplice to the problem?

A wife in such circumstances is faced with a classic paradox. Even if she cuts through the doubt, recognizes her husband for the alcoholic that he really is, she may end up with a hostile and protesting partner who continues to drink. What is more, if she goes "public," openly acknowledging that she is married to an alcoholic, she may end up dealing with the censure or patronizing remarks of acquaintances and neighbors. She may become not just a victim of alcoholism, but a victim of pity too.

On the other hand, if a wife does not face up, does not make that judgment call, what can she then expect?

Let us consider the other side of the situation.

A DISEASE WITHOUT FAVORITES

In the years I have spent treating alcoholics and their families, I have witnessed a depth of pain and suffering that virtually defies description. Alcoholism is a highly democratic disease that does not discriminate between young and old, rich and poor, male and female. It shows no respect for race or religion, or for intelligence, education, or physical stamina.

It is an insidious disease, often gradual and subtle, but capable at any time of exacting hefty vengeance—whether in the way of ill health, criminal irresponsibility, or financial or moral recklessness. Time and again I have seen it strip an otherwise fine individual of pride and purpose, rob him of values and principles, and blind him to what he is doing to himself as well as to those close to him.

In the end, alcoholism takes away health, sanity—even life itself. It leaves behind a trail of wasted opportunities and broken dreams, a family in shambles, the wife and children overwhelmed with feelings of anger, frustration, guilt, shame, and confusion. Perhaps just as painful, the family is often left isolated and alienated in a society that remains relatively insensitive, indifferent, and either uninformed or misinformed about a condition that afflicts so many and affects so deeply the lives and health of those who are close to the alcoholic.

THE DANGER OF IGNORANCE

One client named Muriel refused to accept the possibility that her husband was alcoholic. A heavy drinker, yes—she had no difficulty with this term. But the word "alcoholic" was beyond her. Her reasoning was simple. Her husband made it to the office on time every morning. She was convinced that no alcoholic could do such a thing. Even when told that some 75 percent of all alcoholics are actively employed, she had difficulty accepting this as truth. To her mind an alcoholic was something of monstrous, near-mythic proportions—at the very least a vagabond on a park bench, at most some trembling wretch unable to live without a bottle within arm's reach.

Another woman who came to see me had a similar problem. In her case, the issue revolved around the fact that her husband drank only beer—never wine or hard liquor. Surely an alcoholic would display no such preference. Surely her husband, with his categorical insistence on beer alone (and usually a specific brand), could not really be alcoholic.

Such misconceptions about alcoholism are uncomfortably widespread, and perhaps nowhere more prevalent than among the women who live with alcoholics. Where a wife is concerned, however, to be ignorant is to be at risk. Until an alcoholic is confronted with—or confronts—his disease, the chances of recovery and improvement are practically nil. For a wife this often means only one thing: sustained suffering.

THE FAILURE TO DIAGNOSE

In simplest terms, an alcoholic is a person afflicted with the disease of alcoholism. Such a person cannot necessarily be identified by how much or how little he or she drinks (or even what form of alcoholic beverage); it is what the drink does to the person that provides the clue.

In 1987 the American Psychiatric Association (APA) established three main criteria for identifying the condition known as alcoholism: physiological symptoms, such as hand tremors and blackouts; psychological difficulties, which include an obsessive desire to drink; and behavioral problems that disrupt social or work life.

Even with these and many other guidelines, however, the issue of defining—of specifically pinpointing—alcoholism is still rife with difficulty, for laypeople and specialists alike. One area where this is somewhat visible is the medical profession.

Although alcoholism is officially regarded as a disease and accepted as such by the majority of physicians, it remains underdiagnosed and underidentified. The inability or unwillingness of the medical profession to make the diagnosis of alcoholism can be explained in several ways:

• Alcoholism, as we have noted, is a disease of denial. It is very rare that an individual with a drinking problem will volunteer the fact to anyone, including a physician. Indeed, the opposite is the rule; such individuals tend to mask their problem. They underreport the quantity and frequency of drinking, minimize the consequences, deny getting drunk or experiencing any other kind of alcohol-related problem. They do so partly out of a sense of shame and fear and partly because their perception and self-awareness have been distorted by the effects of alcohol. As a result, physicians are often stonewalled: Even if they suspect that the individual does have a drinking problem, they feel uncomfortable challenging the patient's denial and appearing to suspect him of lying.

• Instead of a single, all-embracing definition of alcoholism or of what constitutes an alcoholic, there are numerous and somewhat vague definitions, each emphasizing different diagnostic criteria. This is partly the result of the sheer diverseness of alcoholism. There is no single identifiable cause and no single symptom or set of symptoms that could identify all alcoholics. No matter which definition a physician might adhere to, certain alcoholics will not be identified by this criterion, and many alcoholics will not have all the characteristics of any specific definition.

• Medical schools and training programs have traditionally failed to emphasize alcoholism in their teaching curricula. The total amount of time a medical student is exposed to the issues of alcoholism is a matter of hours during an entire four-to-five-year program. As a result, physicians are often not very well informed about the diagnosis and treatment of this particularly complex and serious disease.

• Attitudes represent an important factor influencing the underdiagnosis of alcoholism. It may be that the medical profession is simply reflecting the general apathy of society with regard to alcoholism. Several studies have revealed that many physicians do not consider treatment of alcoholism or motivating the alcoholic to accept specialized treatment as their proper role. Part of this is due to the belief that there is no effective treatment available for alcoholism.

WHAT THE DOCTOR SAID

A client named Linda once told me that her husband's drinking had led to many quarrels and difficulties. When she confronted him about his alcoholism he would become infuriated, accuse her of being a nag, and deny that he was alcoholic. He would point out angrily that he did not drink every day, that he had a good job, and that she was well provided for. This kind of argument took place repeatedly.

Finally Linda spoke to the family doctor, explaining the extent of Matt's drinking—his habitual lateness, his occasional shakes, his penchant for sometimes drinking in the morning—and asked what he thought. The physician agreed that there seemed to be a problem. But what could he do about it?

Linda suggested that if he thought Matt was alcoholic and told him so, then maybe Matt would do something about it. The doctor agreed to intervene when Matt came in for his next physical.

Linda spoke to the doctor some weeks after. His comments, she later told me, were: "I think you're worrying yourself for nothing. Matt should be fine now. We had a good talk and he admitted that he sometimes overindulges—but what man doesn't from time to time? Certainly I don't think he has a serious problem. He did seem quite anxious and said that the drinks relax him, so I prescribed some tranquilizers. Otherwise, he's quite okay and in good shape—I don't see him as an alcoholic."

The physician had largely ignored Linda's information about the late-night drinking, the early-morning eye-openers, the occasional shakes. He found no medical symptoms—and since depression was the only condition he could feel reasonably comfortable with, he prescribed antidepressants instead.

The end result was that Matt began to use the medication in combination with alcohol, despite being warned not to. His initial problem was thus compounded, with the risk of cross-addiction thrown in. Finally, one day, Matt decided that he had had enough and abruptly stopped drinking and taking pills. Unfortunately, the sudden cessation of chemical ingestion resulted in a convulsion that required hospitalization. Fortunately Matt did recover and shortly afterward entered a rehabilitation center.

A RAY OF HOPE

Despite the tragedy that befell Linda and Matt, the situation on the medical front is not without hope. Indications are that important changes are taking place. My own experiences and those of many of my colleagues suggest that physicians are beginning to show a much greater interest in obtaining knowledge about alcoholism. I receive numerous referrals from private practitioners, involving patients who need alcoholism treatment. Other physicians have requested technical literature and asked if they can visit our rehabilitation facility to become more familiar with what is going on. Equally promising, a number of hospitals have now established treatment programs for alcoholism and have affiliated themselves with substance-abuse programs. The situation *is* more encouraging—but it is still a long way from where it should be.

Clearly, what is needed is better education for doctors in the treatment of alcoholism and addiction, and better understanding of the vast assortment of indicators so that alcoholics do not block a physician's perception. What also is needed is a readiness on the part of physicians to investigate by asking probing questions of the patient—alcoholism is so pervasive that it should be looked for routinely in the examination of any patient. Physicians should also be more aware of available resources so they can make proper referrals. They should be able to help inform and educate a patient and motivate him to accept treatment.

Instead of looking at this problem in all its seriousness and trying to improve their skills and motivation to deal with it, physicians have too often neglected it. As a result, the problem tends to be repackaged and sent back home. In other words, it becomes once again the wife's dilemma.

ONE MORE DOUBLE STANDARD?

As we noted earlier in the book, wives have traditionally been blamed either for not recognizing a husband's alcoholism or for failing to do something about it. This is very strange. We live in a society in which specialists cannot agree on what exactly alcoholism is, and in which physicians are reluctant or unable to diagnose its presence—yet we choose to fault the wife for *her* lack of understanding of alcoholism, for *her* inability to do something about it.

Why should a wife's underestimation of her husband's drinking not be akin to that of doctors and specialists? Why should it not be attributed to lack of knowledge and lack of information?

Similarly, why should a wife's reluctance to do something about her husband's problem not be attributed to fear of making him angry? The doctor does not make the diagnosis because he does not want to appear judgmental and make the patient hostile. But a wife, who may not want to be accused of nagging and demanding and who may be concerned that her husband's response will be a torrent of verbal or even physical abuse, is not shown the same understanding as the doctor—who in fact has far less at stake in making the diagnosis of alcoholism.

What is more, unlike the physician, a wife risks the shame associated with the stigma of alcoholism, adding further to her reluctance to deal with the issue openly.

It would seem that there is clearly a double standard at work here, two systems of measurement, one that exonerates and exculpates professionals of their helplessness in the face of a tremendously difficult issue, and one that faults the wife for the same thing.

Let us now look at some of the variables that create confusion for anyone—wife especially—trying to pinpoint this disease

A WORLD OF DIFFERENCES

Just as all humans differ, one from another, so too do alcoholics. Some begin drinking in childhood, others during their teens, and still others do not begin until early or late adulthood. (While problem drinking among adolescents and teens has reached crisis proportions in recent years, alcohol abuse is also a primary cause of death and illness among those in the so-called Golden Years of retirement.)

Some individuals drink carefully and sociably for many years and only gradually increase the amount and frequency of alcohol intake until at some point it becomes a problem. Some reach this stage much more rapidly. Some report that they never experienced social drinking, but that they drank heavily from the outset and suffered problems related to their drinking from almost that first occasion. They were never able to have just one or two drinks and feel they had had enough. They were never able to stop when they wanted to, never able to control how much they drank. They were enslaved from the first drink onward.

STYLE OF DRINKING

Just as the onset time of alcoholism varies, so does the manner in which alcoholics imbibe. Some drink steadily and daily. Others hardly drink at all during the week but make up for this during the weekend. There are also those who drink in a very controlled, seemingly nonproblematic fashion—or not at all—for weeks or months, but then go on a prolonged binge.

Some begin in the morning, preferring alcohol to orange juice or coffee. Some never drink before noon. Others may not begin their daily ritual until after work or in the evening.

Some drink only alone, while others seek companionship, and still others are not particular—they will drink alone or with others. Some will sneak and hide their drinks while others do not care and drink openly.

Even more confusing, the same individual may change his pattern of drinking once or several times, going through periods in which his drinking style and behavior appear different.

DIFFERENT DRINKERS, DIFFERENT SYMPTOMS

The results of abusive drinking also vary, for not all alcoholics experience the same symptoms or to the same degree. Some develop physical symptoms requiring medical attention, while others may develop psychological symptoms involving changes in behavior, attitude, or mood. Some alcoholics will experience both types of symptoms. Certain problems will be reversible, others will remain chronic, and still others will be terminal.

There are indications that alcoholism decreases life expectancy ten years or more. Numerous diseases affecting heart and gastrointestinal functioning are also related to the condition. As well, bacterial pneumonia is twice as common among alcoholics, while death from pneumonia is at least three times commoner, and acute gastric hemorrhage is five times commoner than for nonalcoholics. Other ailments range from pancreatitis to anemia to cirrhosis of the liver. Certain unusual diseases of the central nervous system, resulting in symptoms ranging from severe crippling to memory loss, also accompany excessive drinking. On the reproductive front, alcoholic males may develop shrunken testicles, reduced testosterone levels, and even impotence.

Various psychological or behavioral changes also result from excessive drinking. Some alcoholics become physically violent while drinking or withdrawing from alcohol. Some are violent at home, others seem to restrict their violence to outside the home. Some become unreasonably demanding and verbally abusive when not getting their way (or for no apparent reason at all), while others behave just the opposite—they become passive or generous or humorous or just plain retiring. Still others experience sharp and sudden mood swings—one moment joking, the next moment aggressive.

Some show remorse and guilt when they sober up. They become overly generous and conscientious for a period of time; they make promise after promise and beg forgiveness. Others remain steadfastly arrogant, denying any wrongdoing, often blaming the wife for their troubles and misfortune. Some alcoholics develop serious withdrawal symptoms after not drinking for several hours or days. These may include tremors and shakes. The most drastic form of withdrawal, during which an alcoholic may suffer convulsions and hallucinations, is known as delirium tremens, or the DTs. The condition sometimes results in death, and because of its severity is often aptly referred to as "the horrors."

Even ignoring such a bleak fate, however, the overall rate of suicide among alcoholics is significantly higher than among nonalcoholics.

DIFFERENT CONSEQUENCES

Alcoholics differ greatly in the type of social consequences they experience and the degree of seriousness of these consequences. The following is a brief cross section:

- Car accidents
- Arrests due to driving while intoxicated
- Arrests due to being a nuisance, fighting, or other behavior involving disturbance of the peace
- Legal problems
- Financial problems
- Work-related problems (suspension, dismissal, or unemployment, for example)
- Loss of friends
- Health problems
- Marital problems, family problems

In addition, as we have indicated, the course of the disease is not identical in each individual and some alcoholics suffer a much wider range of losses and to a deeper extent than do others. Why this is so is not clearly understood. The prealcoholic health and innate constitution of the individual may certainly play an influential role. As well, an alcoholic may suffer a variety of difficulties, including health, marital, financial, legal, and vocational problems, *well before* he ever begins abusing alcohol—in fact, these may have contributed to his eventual addiction and then served to exacerbate the already existing problem.

What makes one alcoholic so different from another? There are many possibilities; unfortunately there are no definite answers or conclusions. What can be said with fair certainty, however, is that all active alcoholics, regardless of their drinking pattern, will experience considerable difficulty as a result of their addiction. The following poem—author anonymous—makes this point very clear.

On Drinking

We drank for happiness and became unhappy.
We drank for joy and became miserable.
We drank for sociability and became argumentative.
We drank for sophistication and became obnoxious.
We drank for friendship and made enemies.
We drank for sleep and awakened without rest.
We drank for strength and felt weak.
We drank medicinally and acquired health problems.
We drank for relaxation and got the shakes.
We drank for bravery and became afraid.
We drank for confidence and became doubtful.
We drank to make conversation easier and slurred our speech.
We drank to feel heavenly and ended up feeling like hell.
We drank to forget and were forever haunted.
We drank for freedom and became slaves.
We drank to erase problems and saw them multiply.
We drank to cope with life and invited death.

A MULTITUDE OF FACTORS

Recognizing and understanding the differences in cause, course, and effects of alcoholism is of utmost importance, for it enables the specialist—and thus the wife and the alcoholic himself—to see a complete individual whose problems go well beyond just drinking too much or too often. Alcoholism affects the individual's life on many levels, including physical, psychological, marital, social, and spiritual. Whether in treatment or through self-help groups such as AA, the entire person must be addressed, not just one or two aspects of his being. In general, arresting alcoholism is a fairly achievable goal. Even so, if this is all that is accomplished, then very little has happened and the chances of relapse are greatly increased.

Any woman who wants her husband to seek treatment should keep in mind that what is really needed is a movement toward rehabilitation and recovery that means growth and change. Anything less is likely to be short-lived. Arresting alcoholism actually takes only a split second—in other words: yesterday I drank, today I didn't, tomorrow I won't . . . my drinking has been arrested. But recovery is a process that takes a lifetime of commitment and a deep inner desire to stay in touch with who and where one is. There are, unfortunately, no quick, and easy solutions.

QUESTIONS WIVES ASK

Although the foregoing provides only a glimpse of the variables involved in alcoholism, it should be clear by now why many wives are reluctant, initially at least, to pass judgment on a drinking husband. Alcoholism is tricky, and alcoholics—in terms of their disease, the denial it entails, and their desire to get to that next drink—tend to be tricksters.

While many of the wives who arrive at my office are, like Melanie, at first reticent about opening up, with time they begin to ask certain key questions about the nature of alcoholics and alcoholism. Here are some of the most common ones:

What causes alcoholism? The short answer is, no one knows. At present there is insufficient evidence to support the theory that alcoholism is caused exclusively by one factor or another. Alcoholism is more reasonably understood as a multidetermined problem—one that is caused by the interaction of various factors. Recent data clearly suggest that alcoholics may suffer from certain physiological abnormalities, and that there is a hereditary component to the condition. Other research has examined such things as environment, cultural background, climate, societal attitude toward drinking, and even the very price of alcohol—and these factors all seem to have some bearing on the prevalence of alcoholics within a society.

Can my husband be alcoholic even if he doesn't get drunk every time he drinks? It is a common fallacy that alcoholics are always drunk or that they have to get drunk each time they drink. Many alcoholics can occasionally have a drink or two and stop. But the fact that they can occasionally do it doesn't mean that they invariably have control over the amount they drink—they don't.

My husband claims he can quit anytime—surely he can't be alcoholic? Many alcoholics use this tactic to convince a spouse that they have no drinking problem; but a person who has no problem with alcohol does not need to quit or prove anything to anyone. Alcoholics—even those who drink every day—can if necessary stop for a period, using willpower alone. But willpower can generally only take the alcoholic so far and no farther—chances are that sooner or later he will return to drinking and in the same uncontrolled way as he was drinking before he stopped.

My husband claims not to remember certain things he has done while drinking—is he lying? Probably not. Chances are he was experiencing a blackout. Though often mistaken for denial, a blackout is a form of amnesia that blocks out entire sections of time, leaving the alcoholic completely unable to recall events, places, people—or what he did or said.

Does an alcoholic have to "hit bottom" before he can really begin to recover? Alcoholism is often said to be a progressive, deteriorating problem. Certain alcoholics clearly appear to deteriorate in some or many areas and go through progressively more serious stages until they either "hit bottom" or die. But others are able to maintain a certain level for many years. They are drinking alcoholically and there are consequences, but the consequences never seem to go beyond a certain stage or level. A husband, for example, may never lose his job or even get into trouble at work or with the law. There may never be any serious financial or legal complications. But he nonetheless drinks on a regular, steady basis and the marital situation is stressed, unpleasant, and unfulfilling.

Is it true that *some* alcoholics have been cured? Despite claims that have been made about alcoholics who have returned to social drinking, the majority of medical and psychological opinion regards the disease as incurable. Alcoholism can be treated and arrested, however. One way is through specialized therapy. Another way— possibly the most successful method in terms of numbers—is through the AA program.

How can I get my husband to quit drinking? If you ask on a one-to-one basis, you are probably going to run into a brick wall. Chances are there will be denial, then anger, then possibly a bout of even more extreme drinking while your partner licks his wounds—these are stock alcoholic reactions. A more successful possibility is what is called intervention, a technique that is discussed in considerable detail in Chapter 8.

If my husband enters a rehabilitation center, what are the chances of a successful recovery? The best estimates suggest that fewer than 25 percent of patients manage to remain abstinent for three years. While the AA recovery rate is probably higher (between 50 and 60 percent, according to one figure), its record is difficult to assess because of the anonymity of its membership. It should be pointed out, however, that many alcoholics join AA as a follow-up to treatment in a center.

What is AA and how does it work? A fundamental tenet of this million-strong organization is that lifelong abstinence is the only legitimate solution to alcoholism. According to its members, group support is the key to recovery, along with a twelve-step program for learning how to live contentedly without drinking. The program describes itself as "a fellowship of men and women who share their experience, strength, and hope with each other that they may solve their common problem and help others to recover from alcoholism." Regular meetings, anonymity, and a "one-day-at-a-time" philosophy are stressed. There are no fees or dues.

What is Al-Anon and how does it work? Al-Anon works principally in the same way as AA, except it is geared toward those who are being affected by someone's drinking—wives and husbands of alcoholics, for the most part. (See Chapter 10.) A similar organization, Alateen, is especially useful for helping children of alcoholics. There is also now a flourishing network of meetings for ACOAs—Adult Children of Alcoholics.

IS AL-ANON FOR YOU?

Countless millions of individuals are affected by the excessive drinking of someone close. These twenty questions are designed to help you determine whether or not you can benefit from the support of Al-Anon.

1. Do you worry about how much someone else drinks?   Yes   No

2. Do you have money problems because of someone else's drinking?   Yes   No

3. Do you tell lies to cover up for someone else's drinking?   Yes   No

4. Do you feel that if the drinker loved you, he or she would stop drinking to please you?   Yes   No

5. Do you think that the drinker's behavior is caused by his or her companions?   Yes   No

6. Are routines frequently upset or meals delayed because of the drinker?   Yes   No

7. Do you make threats, such as "If you don't stop drinking I'll leave you"?   Yes   No

8. When you kiss the drinker hello, do you secretly try to smell his or her breath?   Yes   No

9. Are you afraid to upset someone for fear it will set off a drinking bout?   Yes   No

10. Have you ever been hurt or embarrassed by a drinker's behavior?   Yes   No

11. Does it seem as if every holiday is spoiled because of drinking?   Yes   No

12. Have you considered calling the police for help in fear of abuse?   Yes   No

13. Do you find yourself searching for hidden liquor?   Yes   No

14. Do you often ride in a car with a driver who has been drinking ?   Yes   No

15. Have you refused social invitations out of fear or anxiety?   Yes   No

16. Do you sometimes feel like a failure when you think of the lengths you have gone to to control the drinker?   Yes   No

17 Do you think that if the drinker stopped drinking your other problems would be solved?   Yes   No

18. Do you ever threaten to hurt yourself to scare the drinker ?   Yes   No

19. Do you feel angry, confused, and depressed most of the time?   Yes   No

20. Do you feel there is no one who understands
your problems?   Yes   No

If you have answered yes to three or more of these questions,
Al-Anon or Alateen may help. You can get in touch with Al-Anon or
Alateen by looking in your local telephone directory.

IS AA FOR YOUR MATE?

AA has aided millions of individuals in achieving and maintaining
sobriety. The following questions are designed to help a drinker
determine whether he or she can benefit from the AA program.

1. Have you ever decided to stop drinking for a
week or so, but lasted for only a couple of days?   No   Yes
2. Do you wish people would mind their own
business about your drinking—stop telling
you what to do?   No   Yes
3. Have you ever switched from one kind of drink
to another in the hope that this would keep you
from getting drunk?   No   Yes
4   Have you had to have an eye-opener upon
awakening during the past year?   No   Yes
5. Do you envy people who can drink without
getting into trouble?   No   Yes
6. Have you had problems connected with drink-
ing during the past year?   No   Yes
7. Has your drinking caused trouble at home?   No   Yes
8. Do you ever try to get "extra" drinks at a party
because you do not get enough?   No   Yes
9. Do you tell yourself you can stop drinking any
time you want to, even though you keep get-
ting drunk when you don't mean to?   No   Yes
10. Have you missed days of work or school
because of drinking?   No   Yes
11. Do you have "blackouts?"   No   Yes
12. Have you ever felt that your life would be better if you did not drink?   No   Yes

Was the answer *Yes* four or more times? If so, this suggests a problem with alcohol.

Key Points

• An alcoholic cannot necessarily be identified by how much or how little he or she drinks (or even what form of alcoholic beverage); it is what the drink does to the person that provides the clue.
• Alcoholics come in an enormous variety of packages, each with a specific drinking style and reaction to drinking. Social and medical consequences of drinking also vary. A similar degree of variability is also found in partners of alcoholics, in terms both of specific reactions to and of consequences from the alcoholic's drinking.
• Alcoholism can be arrested but not cured. Possibly the most successful technique for getting an alcoholic mate into treatment or AA is the procedure known as intervention. This usually requires the aid of an alcoholism therapist or counselor.

Voices: Paul, an alcoholic

WHEN THE SOLUTION BECOMES THE PROBLEM

I started drinking when I was seventeen and I didn't stop until I was forty-one. In other words, almost twenty-four years of my life were devoted to the bottle. She was my mistress, and I was willing to do just about anything for her.

Though I drank hard, I also worked equally hard, and along the way I managed to become a physician, a husband, a father, and a homeowner. At a certain point in my life I had achieved everything I had set out to achieve.

Today things are very different—my wife is happily married, but to another man. I see my children once a week, sometimes twice. My apartment is comfortable, but certainly more modest than the mansion in the suburbs that I once had. And I hope one day to be able to practice medicine again, though the chances are somewhat slim.

I don't quite know how it all slipped through my fingers. It seems that I woke up one morning and everything and everyone was gone—but in truth I know better. I know today that as much as I worked at achieving my dream, I worked even more at creating my nightmare.

It's ironic: When I had everything, I didn't know who I was and I didn't appreciate what I had—I guess I didn't have me. Today I am beginning to get to know who "me" is, and it feels better. Even so, I'm still sad, and I think in a sense I always will be. I hurt a lot of innocent people along the way. I ruined my life and the lives of a woman and four children I loved and still love deeply

It may sound crazy—if I loved them so much, why didn't I do something before it was too late? Why didn't I hear my wife's words when she cried and begged me to get help? Why did it take me so long to recognize that she was right? I suppose the answer is partly that I had the same misconceptions about alcohol and alcoholics that most people have, partly that I believed that I was still in control of my drinking and my life—and partly that I was so desperately afraid to live without alcohol. To ask me to stop drinking forever was a little like asking me to stop breathing forever.

I believed that alcoholics were vagrants and bums, and that certainly a man with a good education, respected in the community and financially successful, could not be an alcoholic. I knew I could stop when necessary, and I proved it on numerous occasions. By stopping, I was able to reassure myself that I was in control—though I was never so much in control that I didn't always go back. In retrospect, of course, I know that all my efforts really proved nothing, because an alcoholic *can* stop for different periods of time—it's just that when he does drink, he can't control the amount. It's like what they say in AA, "One drink is too many, and a million are not enough."

As a physician, I believed I was in the best of positions to know whether I was alcoholic or not, and in my judgment liquor helped me to live more fully—it gave me energy and made me a better doctor. As a recovering alcoholic, I realize now that I was in the worst of positions to know what was happening to me—and that alcohol sapped all the life out of me and turned me into a hopeless quack. Once I had numerous problems, and the bottle was always a solution. Today, the bottle *is* my problem, and there is only one solution—to stay away from it.

Five

How Wives Are Affected

And till my ghastly tale is told
This heart within me burns . . .

—S. T. Coleridge, "The Rime of the Ancient
Mariner"

Throughout most of that first session with Carla, I asked very few questions. I simply listened, sensing that this was what we both needed. Carla needed to talk, to "confess." She was not ready—at least, not yet—to see that her husband's accident had not been her fault. And I needed to listen so that I might come to know and understand the prison she was living in.

Gradually her attention turned to her present situation and what she would do, now that she was alone in the world. I repeated, in a questioning way, "Alone?"

"Well, I mean . . . now that Bob is gone—I mean, I know that I have the kids, but . . ."

"But what?"

"It's just that I'm no good for the kids right now. Alan, my eldest, is ten years old and he misses his father terribly—and what if he blames me?"

"Why would he do that?"

Carla thought for a moment, as though searching for some specific word that would say everything.

"Maybe because I left Bob. . . . I just feel he's so angry—he never hugs or kisses me anymore. He used to love me, you know. . . ."

"And he probably still does. Maybe if you gave him a chance to show it—"

Carla winced, one of the few hints of expressiveness since she had arrived.

"What do you mean, give him a chance?"

"Maybe if you stopped feeling so sorry for yourself and came out of hiding from behind those walls you've erected."

"Feeling sorry for myself? Do you have any idea what it's been like? What I've been through?"

"I can only imagine the hell you've been through," I answered. "But you survived, and not by accident. You survived because of your courage and patience, your perseverance—and most of all, your love. You did everything humanly possible to help Bob recognize what he was doing. You stuck by him, you fought for him, you lied for him, and in the end you even left him for him—in the hope that it would make him wake up and want to fight for his own life."

Suddenly Carla covered her face with both her hands, as though to blot out the exchange. I continued on.

"Carla," I said, "through it all you did whatever you could to remain sane and give the children a warm, stable home. In the end, *everything* wasn't enough—and that hurts. But what you're doing to yourself right now—taking pills, drinking—is worse than anything anyone could ever do to you. You are destroying Carla, you are destroying a very sensible, sensitive, caring human being—for what?"

The hands came away, and tears filled her eyes. She wept copiously, struggling to explain herself.

"I drink to kill my pain. I drink so that I can survive, I drink because my goddam husband destroyed everything that ever meant anything—he destroyed our wonderful family . . . and he's left me all alone to pick up the pieces!" Carla both shouted and sobbed.

"And you're afraid you can't do it," I ventured.

"That's right."

"Well, the Carla I've come to know *can* do it. If you're ready to work at it, I'll help take care of the pain and loneliness of rebuilding your life."

"Oh God, I want to do it . . . but I feel so lost, so afraid to face another day of pain. Please, help me."

THE ISSUE OF LOSS

Alcoholism is not just a disease, it is a process of loss.

For any woman who falls in love with a man who picks the bottle for a companion, life turns into an enormous struggle for survival, a daily effort to minimize the inevitable and mounting losses that surround her and her family.

Just as there is no such thing as alcoholism without consequences, there is no such thing as alcoholism without losses: It is only a matter of time before the different types of losses begin to accumulate. In some cases there is loss of employment, money, property, and other material possessions; in other cases there is loss of friends and family; sometimes there is loss of communication, intimacy, and sharing of feelings; and other times there is loss of hope and finally loss of self, loss of life.

The demands of any intimate relationship are considerable, but when alcohol becomes an active partner, the results are often devastating. It is simply impossible to live with an individual who abuses alcohol and not be profoundly affected by the experience, no matter what the style of that person's drinking. The emotional, mental, and behavioral impact on the wife (and children) tends to be at least equal to the damage suffered by the alcoholic himself—and in some cases even greater.

There is a simple reason for this. While the drinker's perception of reality is distorted and even cushioned by alcohol, and his concerns and anxieties are further diminished by powerful forces of denial, his wife does not enjoy the same "luxury." Unless she herself has begun to rely on alcohol—or tranquilizers, as is the case more often than one might imagine—she does not have the protection of an anesthetic to soften the painful reality of her situation.

The alcoholic may have forgotten or can only partially recall his cruel outburst from the night before, or his embarrassing display of behavior in front of friends, or the crazy, frightening drunken drive home after the party. The wife, however, can remember it all—the events of the previous evening remain clearly imprinted and must be somehow reconciled into her emotional experience.

What is more, a wife is often forced to stand by helplessly while her mate drifts further and further into alcoholic oblivion. She becomes a victim of frustrated impotence. She is left trying, as best she can, to glue together whatever is left of him and their shattered family.

Almost half of all family-court cases are related to alcohol abuse

Alcohol is also implicated in a high percentage of cases involving wife battering, child abuse, and incest. Yet even when these drastic elements are not present, there are other significant difficulties. Alcohol, for example, can adversely affect the drinker's sexual performance by causing transient impotence, which further damages the marital relationship and overall family structure.

One client who came to see me spoke of the revulsion she felt just being in the same bed as her drunken husband. "It was not enough that he was often sweaty and smelly and had stopped caring about his appearance—that was bad in itself. But drinking also turned him into a bed wetter. I was disgusted, thoroughly turned off sexually."

Also, as already indicated, alcoholism can result in serious financial problems as a result of the drinker's impulsive spending or loss of employment, and in legal problems related to traffic accidents and drunk-driving charges. Friends and even relatives of the couple drift away, not willing to put up with this embarrassing or belligerent behavior. While the alcoholic denounces them as boring and no real loss, and replaces them with "drinking buddies," his wife is left feeling ashamed and socially more isolated.

Gradually, as the alcoholic's dependence on alcohol increases, he becomes more preoccupied with drinking and with events that include booze. He may begin to neglect some of his responsibilities as a husband or father. Even if he is physically present, he may be emotionally absent. He often cannot remember what he did or said the day before, and breaks promises and forgets important occasions. His behavior becomes generally inconsistent and unpredictable. One moment he is the kindest person, generous, understanding, and even overly permissive; the next moment he can be unreasonably author- itarian, arrogant, and uncompromising. If confronted about his behavior or attitude, he can become verbally vicious, even physically violent. As often as not, this is swiftly followed by apologies and remorse.

Let us look now at some of the specific effects on wives as a result of living under these conditions.

HOW WOMEN ARE AFFECTED

Although wives of alcoholics may share similar experiences, they are not all affected in the same way or to the same degree. While one woman may feel ashamed, she may not necessarily feel guilty Another, however, may feel shame *and* blame herself for the misfortunes of her family

Again, some women experience anger and frustration as a result of their mates' drinking, while others feel only hopelessness and despair. One woman may feel sad, lonely, and cheated, but she nonetheless presses on with her life Another becomes so depressed and withdrawn that she is unable to function, and in some cases may even choose suicide as an option.

In addition, the same woman may feel differently at various points in the relationship, or she may experience several seemingly conflictual feelings at the same time. For example, Lisa may feel very guilty about her husband's drinking and blame herself for his apparent misery, but at some point she may begin to realize that she did not cause his drinking problem—and the fact that he will not do anything about it leaves her feeling resentful.

Beverly, on the other hand, is worried because it is two in the morning and Stan has not come home or called. Deep down she assumes that he is probably fine, just busy getting sloshed in some bar—he has done this many times before. Even so, she is not sure and feels a nagging concern that something bad may have happened. Finally His Lordship walks through the front door, and Beverly feels relief—but also tremendous bitterness. She begins to berate him, telling him how much she hates him. Stan sits quietly, listening, and then begins to weep, asking her forgiveness and promising to do something about his problem. Beverly starts to feel sad for him—she knows he is sick and not fully responsible for what he is doing. Hate turns to pity, anger turns to compassion. She loves this man and is determined to help him. She begins by helping him out of his clothes.

WHAT DETERMINES HOW WOMEN ARE AFFECTED?

Three main factors determine how the wife of an alcoholic is affected by her partner's drinking. One factor is the type of alcoholic she lives with and the kind of consequences that result from his drinking. A second factor is the wife herself and the vast differences that exist between one woman and another. A third factor is the context in which this is happening.

One could make numerous generalized distinctions—that a middle-aged woman living with a nonviolent alcoholic, for example, will react differently from a young woman living with a violent drinker—but the point is clear. Living with an alcoholic can have a tremendous emotional impact, but the nature and degree of that impact varies from one woman to another.

Among the many emotions brought on by the experience of living with an alcoholic are:

- Shame
- Guilt
- Anger
- Pity
- Fear
- Worry and concern
- Depression

In addition there is the loss of self-esteem, self-worth, and self-confidence, and the development of various psychosomatic illnesses. Let us now look at these points in some detail.

SHAME

Almost all of my clients have talked about embarrassing and humiliating situations that they have found themselves in as a result of their mates' excessive drinking. For Ellen it was a lavish dinner party she had planned for weeks. All the guests showed up, but Frank, her husband, did not. While some of the visitors expressed concern that something must have happened, Ellen knew deep inside that Frank had probably had too much to drink and had forgotten about the event. Eventually one of the guests began to call the various hospitals.

Ellen later described her reaction as this: "I actually found myself wishing that something serious really had happened, maybe an accident or a heart attack. It sounds crazy, but I figured *anything* would be better than his simply being drunk."

Frank did come home late that night, long after everyone had left, drunk and totally oblivious to what had happened. The next day, Ellen telephoned all the guests to apologize, explaining that Frank had passed out from exhaustion and was found by the janitor late at night—and that they were seeing the doctor that morning, that she was very concerned about his health

Another client, named Cindy, spoke about humiliation at a New Year's Eve party when her husband had taken exception to a thoroughly innocent remark. He became verbally abusive, threatening to attack the host. Cindy found herself wishing that the floor would open up and swallow her. Nonetheless she responded in a way that is typical of the resourcefulness of so many wives of alcoholics Despite the fear and anxiety that were welling up inside her, she mustered enough courage and composure to calm her husband and explain to the host and onlookers that this was very unlike him, that he had been under a lot of stress lately.

There are countless other examples of foolish or belligerent behavior that results in deep feelings of shame in a wife. Shame is among the most painful of all the emotions, so powerful it can make a person want to run and hide, to simply disappear It can make an individual feel inadequate, stupid, or a failure

The wife of an alcoholic feels not only ashamed, but also trapped, an alcohostage even in public. She cannot just get up and leave the party; on the other hand, she does not want to stay. She feels hurt, sad, and lonely. She may try to act as if nothing were wrong, or she may try to explain or excuse her husband's behavior, while inside she is falling apart.

We have already noted that isolation is visited on a wife when friends and acquaintances drift away because of the alcoholic's unpredictable behavior. But there is a corresponding dynamic that occurs, inspired by the wife herself. In an effort to overcome the constant sense of humiliation caused by her mate's actions, a wife may attempt to steer clear of any situation that appears threatening, especially social gatherings that involve drinking. As a result she tends to become even more lonely and alienated. In short, she avoids—and is avoided.

A further point about shame is that it is not just brought on by a mate's drunken behavior. Another source is society's attitude toward alcoholics, alcoholism, and wives of alcoholics. Wives, as we have noted, tend to be implicitly and unfairly linked to the husband's illness, whether as cause or accomplice. And despite advances in knowledge about alcoholism, and its official recognition as a chronic but treatable disease, societal attitudes have not kept pace.

Many people still view alcoholism as a self-inflicted problem in a morally degenerate or weak-willed individual. Even among those who say it is a disease, there are those who remain quietly ambivalent. The homeless drunk sleeping on a park bench and the drunk who returns home nightly staggering through the front door are images that have not faded. Though this may be an accurate description of some alcoholics, the majority do not get drunk every day and are not skid-row types—indeed, only 3 percent of alcoholics actually end up on skid row.

So for the wife of an alcoholic the shame is global, the game fixed. She is humiliated by her husband's drunken behavior, and at the same time is ashamed to seek help because of society's negative attitude toward alcoholism. Just as damning, of course, is the prevailing negative attitude on the part of many professionals toward her and her role in supposedly creating her mate's drinking problem or in failing to do anything about it.

She cannot reason with her alcoholic partner, and she cannot share her pain with relatives and friends or even professional therapists.

As a colleague once remarked, "Though she may feel shame, so too should many of us."

GUILT

Stacey was thirty-eight years old and had been married to Rick for twelve years. They had two preadolescent daughters. According to Stacey, Rick had always enjoyed having a drink, especially at social gatherings, and for the first few years of marriage it had never caused her concern. But then several troublesome incidents occurred over a period of months. Once, he became very drunk at a restaurant and could not drive home. On several other occasions he came home late—intoxicated and bruised, apparently as the result of a barroom scuffle. Though she tried to reason with him, nothing much changed.

Eventually, Stacey began to feel alarmed, and accused Rick of being an alcoholic. At this point she threatened to leave him. Rick assured her that everything was fine—it was just a touch of midlife crisis, nothing more. He would be okay. And for a while he was. He came home on time and played with the girls, and the entire family went out together and he hardly drank. Though she was relieved, Stacey also felt guilty for having accosted him about his drinking, for having suggested that he was alcoholic.

But then the drinking began to get out of hand again. This time when she brought it up, Rick became angry, accusing her of wanting everything her own way, of being overly demanding and lacking understanding. Instead of supporting him, she was undermining him.

There was nothing wrong with occasionally getting plastered. He was a good provider and a good father. He never drank in the morning and he never hit her. She had all the material things she could want, and maybe if she were more supportive, he would not need to drink so often.

Stacey recalled that she came away feeling angry but also feeling that he might be right. He had been killing himself at work, and maybe she had not shown enough appreciation, and maybe he needed more understanding—her world was *full* of maybes. Attempting to find a balance, she no longer suggested that they go out together. She kept the children busy when Rick came home from the office and would even prepare a before-dinner drink for him. She continued to cook the meals and keep the house clean, and she made an extra effort to look pretty and be ready anytime he felt like making love. She had begun to accept that his drinking was her fault and that if she changed so would he. But Rick did not change.

Guilt is a sense of feeling personally responsible for something that is blameworthy. Wives of alcoholics often hold themselves accountable for their mate's excessive drinking. Why? Because the alcoholic is an expert at making others feel guilty for his problems. He tends to blame everyone and everything other than the bottle. He blames his boss, the job, his coworkers, traffic jams, the weather. He blames his wife most of all, and blames himself least of all.

Since there is usually a germ of truth in his accusations, the wife begins to think that maybe he is right. Maybe if she became a better wife, he would neither need nor want to drink so much. In reality, nothing could be further from the truth. Alcoholism is a disease, and as long as the alcoholic refuses to accept responsibility for his problem, he will not get better. But his wife, whether she grasps this or not, nonetheless often feels guilty. Some wives feel responsible for having contributed to the drinking problem, while others blame themselves for failing to put an end to it.

When Stacey could finally no longer take the pressure, she went to see her father. She trusted him, believed that he would see her point. Instead he reminded her of how lucky she was to have a husband who worked so hard and provided her and the children with so much comfort. He even suggested that she might have become a little spoiled. Maybe she should give Rick some space. After all, if his drinking was as bad as she claimed, how could he be so successful?

When Stacey finally sought professional advice, the therapist told her that she was an enabler. She explained to Stacey that by taking on extra responsibilities and lessening Rick's responsibilities, she had actually made it easier for her husband to continue drinking.

Everyone, it seemed, agreed that Rick might have some difficulty but that she was the one who either exaggerated or perpetuated the situation. Her husband abused her with his drinking, and her father and therapist abused her in another way. Rather than listening carefully and trying to understand her pain and confusion, one attempted to convince her that her husband was fine and the other showed her how she was actually to blame for the continuation of the drinking problem.

OTHER CONSEQUENCES

Shame and guilt, while principal, are but two of the feelings expressed by many wives of alcoholics. Living with an alcoholic can be frustrating, frightening, and lonely. Many women report that they live in a constant state of anxiety, worried and concerned about everything imaginable .

Such feelings often surface during group therapy. In one session a client named Rena remarked that during her husband's drinking days she would be constantly thinking about what might happen if he lost his job.

"Jerry was drinking so much and for so long that I still don't know how he got away with it. I used to worry constantly—if he got fired, how would we pay the rent and all the other bills? And if he was late in coming home I'd start to worry again—what if he'd had an accident, what if he was dead, what would happen to all of us, how would we survive? Every time the phone rang I'd be afraid to answer, because it might be the police or the hospital or just another bill collector threatening legal action because Jerry hadn't made the payments—which of course he'd sworn he had."

At this point Julie piped in and said that for her it was different— maybe even worse.

"Worry isn't really what I felt—for me it was fear more than anything else. Neil is a very moody man at the best of times, but when he'd go off on one of his binges—look out. He'd come home ready to pick a fight, and if I didn't say anything so as not to anger him he'd explode about that too. And then he'd pick on the way I was dressed, or the way I handled the children, anything. Sometimes he'd get physical, slap me around or push me. Funny, though—I didn't mind it that much, because as long as he was busy with me, he'd leave the kids alone. That was my real fear."

"That's really interesting," remarked Brenda, moving forward in her chair. "I used to worry from time to time, but not that much. And I also wasn't afraid. Garth had always been a good provider and never violent or even vicious. When he'd drink a lot he'd become very funny. He was always the hit of the party, and other women would tell me how lucky I was—and I'd just feel like crying. Sometimes I would actually pity him for the way he was, other times I would pity me. It seemed that he enjoyed the bottle a lot more than he enjoyed me. I felt abandoned, unloved. He never felt like talking much, and he seemed to lose interest in sex—sometimes while making love he'd lose his erection."

Brenda reflected for a moment, then continued.

"Eventually I became very depressed and saw a doctor who prescribed some mood elevators. I just felt even more unlovable. I was convinced that all our problems were due to me. There were days I just couldn't find the energy to get up—I simply had no confidence in myself. But then I found out about Al-Anon, and I've never looked back."

"How do you mean?" asked Rena.

"The most important thing I discovered is that alcoholism is a disease and it has nothing to do with Garth not loving me or my not being a loving wife. I also discovered that other women were going through the same thing I was—and I suddenly didn't feel so all alone. I began to realize that I was normal and not some kind of nut case or neurotic or whatever. Thank God for that. And best of all, Garth is still going to AA and we've begun to feel close to each other again."

Janice was the only one who had not said anything. All eyes turned to her, and finally she spoke up.

"I guess I can identify with all of you—I've felt and experienced all the feelings you've talked about—but I feel trapped. Brad hasn't had a drink in the eight months since he was in the treatment center, but I can't forget what he did to me . . . sleeping with two of my best friends right in our bedroom, and I never knew about it. I think I have forgiven him, but I don't trust him. I know it was alcohol that made him behave that way, but I'm afraid of getting hurt again."

As the session drew to a close, I found myself reflecting on the utter normalcy of the emotions I had witnessed in the room that afternoon.

Do Rena, Julie, Brenda, and Janice sound sick or disturbed? The feelings they have or once had are very reasonable under the circumstances, and not an indicator of pathology. In fact, if a woman living or having lived in any of these situations felt happy, satisfied, or comfortable and went about her life seemingly unaffected by her circumstances, there would be much more to worry about.

CARLA'S FIRST STEP

Aware of the severity of both her physical and mental condition, I decided that before any meaningful therapy could be undertaken, Carla would require medical attention and detoxification. Getting her off the pills and alcohol and stabilizing her was essential. Accordingly, we discussed the matter, and, with her agreement, I made arrangements for her admission to hospital.

Several days later, after completing my rounds on the hospital ward, I dropped downstairs to check on Carla. I recognized an improvement immediately. Her eyes were deep and clear and her voice was much more self-assured. Though surprised, she seemed genuinely glad to see me. She explained that she had spoken to the children, and they sounded really excited to hear from her, and that they were remembering her in their prayers and could not wait for her to come home.

"So much for not loving me." She smiled sheepishly. Then she continued, "I have to tell you that though we had only one session, and though I hardly know you, I somehow feel that you understand me—I feel that you really care."

Her eyes grew briefly moist.

"I guess what I'm trying to say is that I really trust you—and that's something I thought I might never do again."

I reminded Carla that I was no magician and that though I wished I could make all her pain vanish, it was hardly possible.

"It's really in your hands," I said. "It's going to take time and a lot of courage to put together the shattered pieces of your life, but I will be there to give you encouragement."

"I guess that's all I can ask for." She smiled.

Before leaving, I asked Carla if she would mind my sending her a visitor.

"Who?" she wanted to know.

"A very special lady—someone who's been where you are, a member of Al-Anon."

"Al-Anon?" Carla repeated hesitantly. "I've heard about it, but what exactly is involved?"

"Why don't I let her tell you?" I suggested.

Carla nodded. We then arranged our next appointment, to take place after her discharge from hospital.

My impression was that although therapy could help Carla, she would benefit even more from participation in a self-help program such as Al-Anon. My feeling was that by interacting with other women—women who had been through somewhat similar experiences—she would gain not only support and strength, but also love and acceptance, things Carla needed badly.

As I walked back through the hospital corridors, I found myself in a contemplative mood. Yes, I thought, women are affected, often very profoundly, by the alcoholism of a mate. They are affected in many different ways, and Carla's tragedy was just one of them. Although alcoholism may be a disease of denial, it is also a disease of losses. Tremendous losses, the unnecessary losses of life—unnecessary because they need never have occurred. They could have been avoided.

Key Points

• Although all partners are affected by living with an alcoholic, not all are affected in the same way. Introspection and developing a support network of people you can share with will help you understand how and to what extent you personally have been affected.

• Among the many emotions brought on by living with an alcoholic are shame, guilt, anger, pity, fear, and concern. It is important to realize that it is normal to feel these emotions under the circumstances, but that by sharing these feelings you can begin to overcome them.

• Alcoholics can be very adept at blaming their drinking on their partner's behavior. It is essential to keep in mind that alcoholism is a disease, however, and that the person responsible for arresting that disease is the alcoholic himself.

Voices: *Norah, a wife*

CROSSING OVER TO THE OTHER SIDE

My husband died a number of years ago, at fifty-eight. The problem was cirrhosis, and his death plunged me into despair, though I can't say I was surprised—he had been a heavy drinker throughout our thirty-five-year marriage. In the beginning it was mostly beer; in later years it was rum, scotch, just about any hard liquor he could get his hands on. Often he would mix the two: beer for a base, liquor for a chaser.

No, I was not surprised—but it was not until after his death that I really came to view him as alcoholic. Oh, I know, it sounds stupid—almost uncharacteristic really, since I'm a fairly well-read person—but that's the way it was. All the signs were there, of course. He lost his job on two different occasions, in two different towns thousands of miles apart, and each time the issue of drinking was mentioned. My husband denied it, of course. The first time, he claimed that a bottle had been planted in his desk, that it was a conspiracy to force him out of his job (he had a good position, an engineer), and I actually believed him. The second time, the booze issue was only hinted at. The manager came up with some other reason for the dismissal.

Then there was the time—just before he lost the first job—that he was stopped for impaired driving. His license was revoked for that, but again he had an explanation. He had simply blacked out at the wheel and had struck a lamppost; it seemed to be a medical problem. I confess, I was worried and wanted him to see a doctor. He promised he would, but somehow that got lost in the shuffle.

There were other times. Drunk, he would get belligerent. For a period he started to beat me. A couple of times he turned on our teenage son. Yet he was always remorseful after the attacks, and both of us, my son and myself, felt a little guilty despite our anger. One of the reasons, I suppose, was that we recognized he was going through a difficult period. The outbursts followed the loss of his first job, that "unfair" dismissal. You see, in many other ways he had been a good husband and father. He had never been unfaithful to me, he had never been cheap, he had always worked hard. It was difficult not to stick by him when the world seemed to be turning against him.

Anyway, I suppose the question must be, Why didn't I recognize that he had a disease, that he was alcoholic? For that matter, why didn't any of his bosses—or the judge even, when he lost his license—say something in that direction? The answer is that I don't really know. I know that all of this took place quite a few years ago when the word "alcoholism" wasn't quite as talked about as it is now. It's true that I had heard of AA, but I had always had a sort of mistaken view of it—a lot of grizzled men in trench coats, to be frank. Alcoholism just wasn't the kind of thing that happened to people like my husband.

So yes, I suppose the issue was one of ignorance. To have called my husband an alcoholic would have been like labeling him a bum or a deadbeat or some kind of child molester that hung around parks. It was inconceivable that I could think of him in such a way. He was educated, charming at times, and often capable of extreme goodness.

So how did I ever get wise? I actually ended up as a drinker myself. When I first met my husband, I scarcely touched the stuff. But I suppose that living with a constant drinker can affect you in a variety of ways, and in my case—in later years—I simply slipped into the habit of sharing a bottle with him. At first it was just on Friday nights. Then it became on weekends. Finally it became almost every night. The fact is, without that sacred bottle between us, we seemed to have nothing to talk about, we had no life together.

When did I myself become alcoholic? I can't really say. I don't think it was there at the beginning; it was like a line I crossed one day. Certainly, after my husband's death, after I had lost my best drinking partner, things became unbearable. And unmanageable.

In some ways I became more vicious than my husband, more angry, more filled with self-loathing—I suppose I hated the world for a while. Who knows what makes an alcoholic? Who knows if one alcoholic can produce another alcoholic? Who knows if I would have been alcoholic had I not met my husband? To my mind, alcoholism is probably a thing that lies dormant in some people, and if the right opportunity is there, the right environment—such as a drinking husband—well, maybe it just comes out. That's something for the experts to find out.

All I really know is that it happened to me, and that maybe I would have gone the same way as my husband had my son not intervened. A couple of years after my husband's death, when I was deep in the throes of alcoholic despair, my son arrived at the apartment one afternoon. Everything was in a mess. There were clothes everywhere, plates, empty glasses, empty bottles, the works. And as for me, I looked like a dog's breakfast, to be frank. I don't think I have ever seen my son so angry and hurt. He began to scream terrible things at me. At first he began using words like "lush." Then finally the right word came out. He called me an "alcoholic."

I got help at AA a little after that. I've never really looked back since—and maybe that's because I'm afraid to. If I look back too hard, I may have to examine all the sadness, the failure, that comes from not having recognized my husband's alcoholism in the first place. I loved him, you see.

Six

How Wives Respond

... she sacrifices, adjusts, never gives up, never gives in, but never forgets.

—The Rev. Joseph L. Kellerman,
*Alcoholism: A Merry-Go-
Round Named Denial*

I did not hear from Melanie for almost four months, but one evening as I was preparing to leave the office the telephone rang. The voice on the other end was that of a very sad and nervous-sounding man. He introduced himself and said that his wife had been a patient of mine about four or five months previously.

It took a moment or so for me to recall the subdued blond woman who had dreamed about whirlpools and who had apologized for weeping like a child.

"Of course," I said. "How is Melanie?"

There was a brief silence, a clearing of the throat.

"I'm afraid things are not very good," said Mike.

"Oh?"

There was a hesitancy in his voice as he attempted to explain.

"A week ago she took some pills," his voice cracked. "I guess she was trying to kill herself," he said.

"How is she now?" I asked.

"She's fine," said Mike. "She's still in hospital, but I expect she'll be released in the next few days."

Mike then went on to say that he and Melanie had been talking a great deal since the incident, and that they had reached a decision to seek therapy together. They needed help. Would I consider taking them on?

"Of course," I said. We agreed to meet the following week.

A LOVE STORY

The relationship between an alcoholic and his bottle is a little like the relationship between a man and his mistress. It may begin innocently enough—lighthearted talk, occasional flirting, and so on. Pleasant times, nobody is hurt. At first he enjoys the casualness of this relationship; he feels good, he feels relaxed. But gradually the relationship begins to take on more serious overtones. He prefers to stop at the bar after work rather than go directly home—he feels he needs to spend more time talking with this new and beautiful seductress. In her presence he feels warm and secure and important.

Gradually he begins to spend more and more time with her—though he has been seduced, he does not yet see it. He sets out at noon hour to see her, and his lunches extend into the afternoon and sometimes evening. Eventually he finds that he is even craving her in the morning, and so he drops in to see her. Occasionally he goes away for an entire weekend, ostensibly on a fishing trip; instead he spends the whole time in his new mistress's arms.

His wife has by now become suspicious and concerned. She confronts him about his behavior and even accuses him of having an affair. He denies it, admitting only that he has a companion whom he likes and enjoys talking to and, yes, maybe he has been spending a little too much time with her but that it is all very innocent and there is no need for concern. In fact, to prove to his wife and to himself that he really is in control, he does stop seeing her. He comes home early each day, and shows renewed interest in his family and especially in his wife.

His wife feels relieved and reassured, in fact a little guilty and ashamed for having mistrusted him. After a week or so of good behavior, however, he begins to feel edgy; he misses his companion terribly and is anxious once again to spend time with her. Finally one afternoon on his way home from work he drops in to see her, intending only to visit for a few minutes. But the road to Hell is paved with good intentions, one word leads to another, and he soon loses all sense of time. Before he knows it, it is dawn and he never made it home. Even worse, he is now really hooked on his mistress.

This time when his wife confronts him about his behavior, he becomes resentful, accusing her of being a nag and a shrew. Perhaps if *she* changed her attitude and improved her appearance, he might feel more inclined to come home instead of spending time with his companion. As angry and as hurt as his wife feels, she begins to think that maybe he is right. Maybe if she took more care of her appearance, maybe if she looked more sexy, he wouldn't be craving that other woman.

She tries everything in her power, not realizing that whatever she does will not change anything, because her husband's relationship with his mistress is not a mere flirtation, it is an addiction. She cannot possibly give her husband what his mistress is able to give him. When he is in his mistress's grasp he becomes Superman. He feels tough, confident, knowledgeable on every topic. He knows what is wrong with society, and who the Rangers should trade and why—he even knows how to run the country better than any president or prime minister. He forgets his problems and feels as though he has no worries in the world. It may all be a delusion—but for those few precious hours he feels on top of everything. How can his wife replace such a wonderful mistress? What can she offer him in exchange? Reality? Reality is what he is trying to escape.

In the end the alcoholic begins to pay a very heavy price for his relationship with his mistress. His friends have begun to drift away, his health has been affected, his job may be on the line, his marriage is almost destroyed, and he has financial problems, but he continues to deny that any of this has anything to do with her. Though he is afraid of losing his job, friends, and family, he is even more afraid of facing life without his trusted companion.

In the interim, his wife tries to hold the family together. Though she feels shattered, neglected, and abandoned, she continues to do whatever is necessary to survive. As he ignores more and more of his responsibilities, she takes over, attempting to make ends meet. She may have considered leaving him on numerous occasions, but for various reasons has remained. By now she may have realized that some of this is her fault, but she knows he is sick and hopes that somehow he will face reality and again be the man she was once passionately in love with. Meanwhile, when others ask if anything is wrong, she says no, everything is fine. She is *not* denying reality—

simply put, how can she say otherwise? She is too ashamed to admit that her husband, the man she lives with, is hooked on another woman.

RESPONDING TO THE PROBLEM

Women respond to a husband's alcoholism in a host of different ways. Melanie's bid at suicide is one extreme. Carla's decision to leave is another way of responding. Some women use indifference as a means of pressuring a husband to stop drinking, and others try to browbeat him into quitting. While some wives seek solace in clandestine affairs, others—like the wife in the previous story—make efforts to enhance their sexuality and "seduce" the husband away from the bottle, and still others withhold sex in an effort to get the husband to quit. Some women hide or empty the husband's bottles, others steal his drinking money.

Depending on the relationship, any of these tactics may conceivably have some effect in getting an alcoholic to quit. They are just as likely, however, not to work. A woman who offers a choice between sex and the bottle should not be surprised to find that her husband opts for the bottle. A woman who steals her husband's drinking money should not be surprised to discover that he catches on quickly and begins to place his *real* drinking money in another pocket. A woman who empties her husband's bottles into the sink should not be surprised to find an armada of other bottles waiting to replace them. A woman who tries to seduce her husband away from drink should not be surprised to find out that while love is said to conquer all, alcoholism may prove to be an exception. Even indifference or constant arguing can become the fuel that inspires the alcoholic—in his own mind, at least—to drink. "She doesn't love me" is the way it goes. "She doesn't understand me" is the way it goes.

In the alcoholic's drunk and distorted mind, everything and everyone is to blame for his misfortunes, except for himself and least of all alcohol. But what is even more disturbing is that almost any and every effort his wife makes to adjust and cope with his behavior is perceived as a symptom of psychological illness in the eyes of many sober, clear-minded professionals.

If she is frustrated and angry because her husband will not do anything to help himself, or if she argues or nags or begs or cries for him to stop drinking, she is said to be *hostile* or *overly aggressive*.

If she attempts to ignore his behavior and avoid argument or confrontation, she is said to be *uncaring* or *unloving*.

If she tries to maintain an outward appearance of well-being or pretends that circumstances are not as bad as they seem, then she is accused of *denial* and of being as sick as—or sicker than—her alcoholic mate.

If she takes over responsibilities that her mate is neglecting, or borrows money to pay the bills and debts, then her actions are regarded as indicative of an underlying need to *control* and *dominate* a weak, ineffectual man.

If she lies to her husband's employer, saying that her mate is sick when he is in fact suffering a hangover, she is described as *covering up*.

If she explains to friends that her husband's foolish or belligerent behavior at the party the night before was uncharacteristic and a result of being stressed and overworked, she is accused of *defending* him.

If she avoids social gatherings where there is drinking, she is considered to be *protecting* him.

If she decides to stay with her man for any of countless reasons, it is cited as proof of her *masochism* or underlying need to suffer.

In short, no matter how a woman attempts to deal with her husband's alcoholism and its effects, her behavior is interpreted in negative terms. She is viewed as being either a disturbed personality purposely seeking a relationship with an alcoholic man, or a normal personality that became disturbed as a result of living with an alcoholic man, or an enabler, itself an indication of being sick.

THE QUESTION OF NORMAL

Given the foregoing, then, is there nothing a wife can do that might be considered as normal, appropriate, acceptable behavior in view of the so-very-abnormal, stressful conditions in which she finds herself trapped?

Maybe if she chose not to stay in such a relationship? No chance—if she left him, her action would most likely be interpreted as abandonment of her mate when he most needed her, and thus further evidence of her underlying hostility toward men.

Such an interpretation would certainly be consistent with the generally negative perception shown by professionals toward wives of alcoholics. As a colleague once remarked, "Far too many of us sit back and observe the behavior of these women, offering up statements and comments that are judgmental but not necessarily helpful."

ARMCHAIR QUARTERBACKS

To echo my colleague's sentiments, it is easy to be an armchair quarterback and second-guess someone else's decisions. If a woman lies to her husband's employer about his hangover and this is defined as protecting or covering up—even worse, as enabling him to drink and deteriorate further—then what are we suggesting? That if she were a "healthy" woman, rather than a disturbed coalcoholic or enabler, she would tell the employer the truth?

If she tells the employer the truth and her husband reacts violently against her and the children, then what? If as a result of her telling the truth the employer suspends or fires the husband and the entire family is thrown into financial crisis, then what? Are the therapists paying the rent or feeding the children?

Rather than criticizing and judging the wife's behavior, it would be far more effective to try to understand the context of her behavior and what options she really has, and what type of social services and mental or emotional support she truly requires and can benefit from.

A LEGITIMATE RESPONSE?

Based on what tends to be said about women married to alcoholics, it would seem that the only legitimate response for a wife is to seek therapy. She is supposedly a sick person, in need of professional help.

Unquestionably, there are people in the general population who suffer from various forms of psychological disturbance, and undoubtably some of these are women who marry men who are or become alcoholic. How this affects and further complicates the marital relationship is an important and justifiable question. However, many, many more women who become involved with alcoholics were not emotionally disturbed prior to the relationship and do not suffer from any identifiable illness as a result of such a relationship. Nonetheless they are certainly *affected* by the experience just as any normal human being would be.

A person who loses a loved one as a result of separation, rejection, or death can most assuredly be expected to go through a period of grief, depression, anger, or bitterness. Some may even experience a profound loss of interest in the pleasures of life, contemplate suicide, or temporarily deny that the loved one is gone. An individual living through such a crisis can often benefit from some form of emotional support and understanding, and may even require professional care. But this does not mean that he or she is psychologically disturbed. If every person who contemplated or required psychotherapy were considered to be emotionally ill there would be very few humans who could claim to be sane or normal.

To feel ashamed when your mate makes a drunken fool of himself or you in front of others is normal. To want to hide or disguise his drinking problem in a society where there is still such stigma associated with alcoholism is understandable. To feel worried and concerned about what is happening to a person you love makes at least as much sense as feeling angry and bitter that he cannot seem to stop drinking or keep his promises.

Choosing to take care of an alcoholic mate and also screaming in frustration are natural human responses under the circumstances. Maybe lying to a boss or not admitting the truth to a friend *is* enabling—but not the kind of behavior that enables him to drink. It is the kind that allows a wife and children to survive in circumstances that are sometimes unbearable.

I am not suggesting that all or any of these responses or coping techniques are good, correct, or effective. What I am saying is that they are not abnormal or pathological. It is natural to cry when you are hurt, and to smile when you are pleased. Life with an alcoholic partner is unstable, unpredictable, and sometimes completely chaotic. To be emotionally affected is normal and to be expected.

MELANIE AND CARLA

Melanie and Carla are examples of two women who shared very similar experiences but were affected differently and reacted differently to their particular circumstances. Both women were about the same age, and each had young children. They were both married to alcoholics who were successful professionals. Neither man abused the children. Both men enjoyed drinking, but neither appeared to have a problem when first married.

In Melanie's case, her husband's drinking began to change just after the birth of their first child. Melanie was absorbed with the baby and eventually with a second child, and it was only later—after Mike began to stay out late—that she became aware of how far she and her husband had drifted apart. When Melanie tried to confront the problem, Mike attributed his drinking to job stress, financial pressure, and Melanie's lack of understanding. Melanie accepted much of the blame and tried to change her behavior and appearance, but the relationship did not improve. The problem was that Mike was becoming dependent on alcohol and Melanie was unable and unwilling to see this. No matter what adjustments she made, it would not change his need for alcohol.

Melanie felt angry but also blamed herself for the loss of intimacy and communication. Though she recognized her husband's increased drinking, she did not see it as an alcohol problem but as Mike's disappointment in her as a wife and woman. When all her efforts did not bring about change, she became despondent and began to develop a variety of psychosomatic symptoms, including stomach pain. She sought help from a physician for her physical symptoms but continued to deny that her husband had a drinking problem. She was convinced that whatever was wrong was somehow due to her.

In Carla's case, Bob's drinking did not change at a given point in time; it was gradual. Carla became aware at some point that Bob's behavior had changed. Several times he got drunk and acted foolishly in front of friends, saying things that humiliated her. Carla responded by confronting her husband about his drinking, and when he blamed it on work and her demanding attitude, she did not accept blame. For Carla it was clear that her husband's drinking was the problem.

Over the next year or two there were many quarrels. Carla threatened to leave, and Bob improved, but only briefly. Despite the threats, Carla was reluctant to leave. She loved Bob and felt she could help him. He had always been a kind person, and when not drinking he still was. He was also a good provider, and they lacked very little in material things. Their love life, intimacy, and communication, however, had seriously deteriorated—and eventually it became evident that she could not help him if he would not help himself, and that leaving was necessary for the preservation of both herself and the children.

DIFFERENT PERCEPTIONS

Melanie denied her husband's drinking problem. She blamed herself, felt guilty and responsible. Carla recognized Bob's drinking problem. She did not feel responsible for causing it, but accepted responsibility to help him stop. When that failed, she tried to back off—and that did not work either

Why did these women react differently? Partly because they are two different women. They perceived the problem differently and interpreted it differently. It became apparent later in therapy that Carla was a much more secure individual than Melanie. She had more confidence and a greater sense of self-worth.

Melanie had grown up with an alcoholic father and what she described as an ineffectual mother. She had always felt that if her mother had been a better wife, then maybe her father would not have become alcoholic. She grew up determined not to make the same mistake. She also grew up with a specific concept of what an alcoholic was—her father, drunk almost every day, often unemployed and sometimes violent. Mike had a good job, was not drunk every day, and was never violent, so he could not be alcoholic. The problems in their relationship were—in her mind, at least—probably due to her ineffectiveness, the shortcomings she had always seen in her mother. In the end Melanie did not have parents she could rely on and turn to for advice and support.

Carla grew up in what might be described as a normal, warm environment with no drinking problem. When Bob's behavior changed and she noticed the connection between that change and his drinking, the conclusion was clear. She tried different approaches— reasoning with him, quarreling and threatening, taking over responsibilities, and finally backing off and detaching. In the end Carla had a strong family support system and parents she could turn to.

Though neither woman could be described as psychologically disturbed, each dealt with her problems in a somewhat different manner and each was able to benefit from psychotherapy and participation in a self-help group.

The fact is there is no "best" way to respond to or cope with an alcoholic partner. In some cases leaving will result in his stopping his drinking, in other cases he will begin to drink more, and in some cases he will drink himself to death or commit suicide.

Sometimes where the wife tries to reason with her husband, while protecting him by lying to the boss, making excuses for his drunken behavior, and taking over responsibilities at home—all the while continuing to quarrel with him over the bottle—the husband will finally join AA or go for treatment.

There are perhaps only two reasonably tried-and-true responses that a wife should consider when grappling with the issue of alcoholism. One, as we have mentioned, is professional intervention (see Chapter 8). The other is to forge some sort of life for herself, independent of the drinker. This implies establishing or maintaining a support system of friends—including, for example, members of Al-Anon.

THE MYTH OF DENIAL

Denial has been cited as one of the major obstacles to a wife's effectiveness in coping with an alcoholic mate. It is important, however, to separate real denial from apparent denial. The difference is subtle but significant. For although denial is indeed one of the prime characteristics associated with wives of alcoholics, it is also one of the prime examples of how these women have come to be misunderstood, and of how easily myths are created and perpetuated.

There are many problems with the concept of denial, not the least of which is the nonchalant manner in which it is applied wholesale to women married to alcoholics. The wife's denial has frequently been seen as identical to that of the alcoholic. Just as the drinker denies his alcoholism, so does his wife deny the problem. But is this true? Are we talking about the same thing?

Denial has various meanings which, without clarification, can result in confusion. In the psychiatric context, denial is a psychological defense mechanism that permits an individual not to become aware of some aspect of reality that would cause fear or anxiety or conflict. The denial continues even after the individual has been given information that should refute the denial.

On the other hand, being aware of something and refusing to acknowledge it to others or knowingly refusing to admit the truth is *not* denial in the psychiatric sense.

If a woman gives birth and the baby dies and she is made aware of what occurred but continues to speak of her child as if he or she were still alive, this is denial.

Similarly, if an individual is told by his physician that he must stop drinking because it is killing him, and yet he still continues to drink, insisting that alcohol is not a problem, this also is denial.

However, if a husband drinks too much too often and makes a fool of himself at social gatherings and people ask his wife what is wrong with her mate and she insists that he is just tired or under stress (while knowing full well that drinking is the problem), this is not denial—it is simply unwillingness to admit the truth—or choosing to keep her personal affairs private.

In everyday language, of course, this is also called denial—but it is very different from denial in the psychiatric context. The distinction is not just a question of semantics. It has important implications.

DENIAL AS A COPING MECHANISM

Denial in the psychiatric context is an indication of some emotional illness that may require psychological intervention. It is a symptom of underlying disturbance. The other form of denial, however, is not necessarily symptomatic of any kind of illness and does not require psychological intervention.

There are various reasons why women may choose not to acknowledge a drinking problem in their mate. They may feel ashamed and concerned about how it will reflect on themselves and their children. They may want to protect the family from outside gossip or ridicule. They may initially feel they can solve the problem quietly and within the immediate family. They may simply not know what alcoholism is, or they may have a misconception of what it is.

This does not represent denial and therefore is not an indicator of underlying psychopathology and does not require treatment. A woman in this situation may need help—but of an educational, informational, and supportive nature.

I am not suggesting that wives of alcoholics never experience psychiatric denial or that any observed so-called denial is always nothing more than a decision not to admit the truth. What I am saying is that too many sweeping generalizations in this area have given denial an almost mythlike status where wives of alcoholics are concerned.

In my years of dealing with these women, I have noted that the vast majority knew for a long time that their mate had a serious drinking problem and some even knew he was alcoholic. They attempted to cope with the situation in countless ways, including confronting their mate. At the same time they did not volunteer the information to anyone and did not acknowledge it even to relatives when questioned.

Each woman had her own particular reasons for doing so, and many of the reasons were common to a lot of women. Many of the women, in retrospect, did not pretend that the way they handled the situation was the best way or even a good way, but the issue was most assuredly not one of denial. It merely looked that way

In simplest terms, then, when an individual consciously chooses to deny, chances are it is not a symptom of psychological disturbance. The warning light is for when we are *unaware* of denial. Even so, we all tend to employ a certain amount of denial, especially when faced with real or perceived extreme danger or stress. Temporary denial can be a healthy, helpful, adaptive way of coping with situations that are or appear to be overwhelming. It gives an individual the opportunity to pull back and regain energy without experiencing paralyzing panic. If we did not sometimes deny certain realities we might all be prone to serious mental-emotional breakdown.

AFTER THE CRISIS

It was late afternoon when Melanie and Mike arrived at my office. Mike appeared first, holding the door open for Melanie to enter. He was well-dressed, in a conservative suit and tie, and had dark hair and somewhat boyish features. There was a touch of shyness in his demeanor, but he nevertheless seemed self-assured. As he identified himself, he smiled affably.

For some reason, Mike's appearance held few surprises for me. He was pretty much the way I had imagined him. But Melanie looked terrible. Not only did she seem to be in complete contradiction to her well-groomed husband, she seemed also to be in complete contradiction to the somewhat polished and confident woman who had first come to my door four months earlier. She was a shadow, a faint image of the child-woman I had initially encountered.

Though her clothes—green slacks and blouse—were tidy enough, they seemed somewhat drab and ill-fitting. Her face too seemed to reflect this fact. It was pale and downcast. There were deep circles beneath her eyes, and it was clear that she had made only the barest of efforts to apply makeup. She looked remote and as if all the life had been drained from her body. Of course, given what she had evidently just been through, it was not surprising.

We exchanged greetings briefly, and Melanie and Mike took seats opposite. There was a long silence during which nothing was said. I waited, allowing the silence to linger, allowing both to get comfortable with their thoughts, but still nothing was forthcoming. After several more seconds, I finally spoke.

"Well," I said. "Who would like to begin?"

Key Points

• Wives and companions employ a variety of coping techniques when living with an alcoholic. Sometimes these actions work; often they do not. While failure may lead to feelings of inadequacy, it is important to remember that whatever was done was done in order to survive and to get the alcoholic to stop drinking. There is no shame in this.

• There are perhaps only two reasonably tried-and-true responses a wife should consider when grappling with a husband's alcoholism. One is to forge a life for oneself, independent of the drinker, and involving some sort of support network. The other is professional intervention, discussed in Chapter 8.

• Though you may have been accused of denying your partner's drinking problem, there is a great deal of misunderstanding attached to this notion. Real denial among wives of alcoholics is relatively rare. Denial, in the sense of knowing the truth but not wishing to share it for various good reasons, is not denial in the psychiatric sense and is not generally an indication of psychological disturbance.

Voices: Jill, a daughter

A QUESTION OF OPTIONS

People say mothers get the blame for everything in this world. As far as I can see, mothers married to alcoholics get it worse. I'm twenty-six now, happily married to a man who prefers sports to drinking—thank God! Growing up was a different story. For the first sixteen years of my life my father was a pain, my mother a complete bag of nerves. My twin brother and I were somehow expected to come out of this unharmed, which of course didn't happen. He got hooked on drugs for a long time, though he's off them now, has been for several years. My own journey was a little different, a sort of whirlwind tour of half the shrinks in town. But I'm okay now—I believe I am, at least.

What is strange is that my father—on the surface, at least—wasn't the real problem. He quit drinking when I was sixteen, and I was proud of him, though it took me a while to trust him again. The bigger problem was my mother. It took years to come to grips with her role in the whole situation. I was inclined to blame her, and it was a blame that was filled with anger. For a long time I couldn't even speak to her. She was, after all, the sober adult in the relationship. Why did she just stand back and let him drink for so long? She seemed so oblivious to it all, and especially to us kids, who were really suffering. I thought she must be incredibly weak and uncaring.

As I said, I worked my way through half the therapists in town. There was one who got me completely confused, made me feel I was all wrong and my parents were saints: "Hey, your dad beat the bottle, your mom rode it out with him—there's a love story in there." You think I was ready for that, after all the crap? An optimist the guy was, and *obviously* not from an alcoholic home.

But there was another—a great guy!—who managed to pull me around. I started, for once, looking at my mother not as some kind of machine that was supposed to do just what I expected, but as a human. A person. I began to see that what I called choices were actually—can I use the psychologist's expression?—limited options. If she went left, she was going to bang into a brick wall. If she went right, she was going to drown. And all the time, in her own weird way, she was taking us into consideration, trying to cope with my father's drinking as best she could, trying to keep us all together. It's just possible that the middle road is the best or only road, if you know what I mean. . . .

But there's a happy ending. Finally, I began to see it differently, that my mother too had been damaged, that she was hurting badly—just like me, just like my brother, just like our father.

One evening, when I finally understood this, I invited Mum out for supper. We talked long and hard. I ended up crying, unable to believe how much she really did love me, how she had done all these strange things—sacrificed herself, really—because of our family. You know, they say God works in mysterious ways; so do mothers in alcoholic families.

I hate to say it: We actually got a little bit drunk—tipsy, really. First we were laughing, then we were crying, then we were laughing again. We held hands almost all evening long, comparing memories. I want to take that back, what I just said. Neither of us got drunk, we just got happy.

I don't think you'll ever see me drunk, or my mother. We know too much about the other side of it. You will see us happy, though, from time to time, in a restaurant. We go out together a fair amount now. Some people think we're nuts, this crazy laughter. But I don't care. We have a lot of laughing to catch up on.

Seven

Mothers and Children

Happy families are all alike; every unhappy family is
unhappy in its own way.

     —Leo Tolstoy, *Anna Karenina*

The experience of growing up with an alcoholic father and an
ineffectual mother had given shape to many of Melanie's beliefs and
attitudes about herself, her marriage, and family life in general. It had
filled her with repressed memories, with guilt, with feelings of
inadequacy and failure, with an overwhelming belief that whatever
was wrong in her family was largely her fault and largely hers to fix.
During that first joint session, these past experiences could be clearly
seen as a central factor in her present marital situation.

Melanie was the first to open up. She appeared nervous, and there
was a tremor in her voice. As she spoke, Mike sat rigidly, staring at
the floor, avoiding any eye contact. She began slowly and cautiously,
first apologizing for what she had done and expressing concern about
how badly she must have frightened Mike and the children.

"I just don't know what triggered it. I had never thought about
killing myself, and I don't think I really intended to when I took all
those sleeping pills. It's just that something came over me."

"Can you be more specific?" I asked.

"Well, I guess things just accumulated. Our relationship was not going that well—Mike and I were just getting farther and farther apart. I tried to do something about it—actually, I tried a lot of things to help him—but we just ended up having more arguments about his drinking and then he'd storm out and drink even more. I began to feel really useless. I felt Mike no longer needed me or wanted me—"

"But you know that's not true," Mike interjected. "How many times have I told you how desperately I need you? How much I love you?"

"Yes, that's what you tell me—but you have a funny way of showing it. You don't anymore. You used to be so loving, you were truly my Prince Charming. But you've changed, I no longer know who you are. One day you're kind and caring, then just as suddenly you become a tyrant, a sort of Jekyll-and-Hyde. You say the most vicious things. And now you've even started throwing things and breaking dishes and glasses—and sometimes I think I'm next."

"You *know* I'd never touch you or the children."

"I know that when you're drinking you're probably capable of anything—and what is worse, you don't even remember the next day what you said or did."

"Frankly," said Mike, with a sigh, "I think you're exaggerating. Sure I lose my temper sometimes—who doesn't? But I'm not out of control, the way you like to put it. I'm telling you it's that crazy family of yours who messed up your head."

There was sudden silence.

Finally I turned to Melanie and asked: "What are you thinking?"

She waited a moment before answering.

"Well, I guess Mike has a point. I know that the afternoon before I took the pills I was just sitting by myself and crying. Then Philip, our eldest, came home, and he asked what was wrong. I told him nothing was wrong. Then he said, 'Why don't you stop acting that way? You're always crying or screaming, you're making us all miserable—no wonder Dad drinks so much.' "

Melanie began to sob again.

"I felt like a knife had just gone through my heart," she murmured.

At this point, Mike put his arms around Melanie, assuring her that it was not really her fault. The words had no effect, and Melanie continued speaking:

"I thought about it all the rest of the afternoon, and I realized that not only was I useless to Mike, but the kids hated me too. And where were my friends? They all seemed to have left me. Suddenly I saw that I had become just like my mother—a totally hopeless, useless object. And then I thought that everyone would be better off if I were dead. And then later in the evening, there was another incident. . . ."

DAUGHTERS OF ALCOHOLICS

Like many children of alcoholics, Melanie was inclined to be an approval-seeker. Growing up, parenting two dysfunctional parents, and often feeling vaguely to blame for the situation, she desperately sought that rare pat on the head, the fleeting smile that said, "You've done well." It was a trait that was deeply embedded, and one that was not likely to go away without help.

Approval, for many children of alcoholics, confirms their sense of self-worth. To a large extent, they derive their identity from gratifying the needs of others, rather than focusing on their own needs. At times, because of this neglect of self, their emotional range tends to be limited.

Maybe more so than other children of alcoholics, eldest daughters are often inclined to be competitive and highly competent. Counterbalancing this, however, is a nagging sense of worthlessness. Sometimes, later in life, this amounts to a feeling of sexual inadequacy, sometimes a feeling of inadequacy as a wife or mother. The overall result of these two polarities is emotional ambivalence.

Need for control is another facet common among children of alcoholics. Because they have been let down so often in childhood, because they perceive that they are surrounded by inadequacy, they feel obliged to adopt a take-charge position at all times—no one else can really be trusted. As a result, they often have trouble asking for help, and indeed trouble asking for anything at all. This difficulty was somewhat evident the first time Melanie came to see me, the way in which she seemed so uncomfortable, even apologetic for troubling me, and then her resistance to go on with therapy.

On the surface, many children of alcoholics appear perfectly all right but are often extremely unhappy. Many contain a great deal of suppressed anger, and this sometimes funnels its way toward the partner. If the partner is alcoholic, the person's drinking provides a convenient focus for the anger. If the partner is not alcoholic, however, much of the anger tends to be blunted and therefore becomes self-directed. This leads to a certain distancing from others, and strong feelings of emotional alienation.

All of the foregoing considerations needed to be taken into account when assessing the situation between Melanie and Mike. But there were other issues too.

FORGOTTEN CHILDREN

No one really knows how many children of alcoholics there are in this world, but the number is certainly colossal. In North America alone it has been estimated that there are more than 25 million, either children presently living with one or more alcoholic parents, or adults who once grew up in such a home. Yet it is only recently that researchers have begun to take serious note of the magnitude of the problem and to assess the emotional effects of being raised in what, all too often, is a terrible and soul-destroying environment.

For years it was assumed that children, like spouses of alcoholics, were somehow immune to the drinker's dependency on alcohol, or that if they were affected the effects would somehow magically disappear once the alcoholic stopped drinking. It was not until the late 1960s, however, when Margaret Cork published her insightful and touching book about children of alcoholics, *The Forgotten Children*, that it began to filter through that offspring can be—and often are—profoundly affected by the various experiences of living with an alcoholic parent.

Gradually we have come to realize that not only are these children vulnerable, but even after they have grown up, moved out, and gone on with their lives there is often a significant residue of pain and difficulty left over from childhood.

What happens to children of alcoholics? What kind of difficulties do they continue to experience as adults? Why are some affected much more severely than others? And, equally important, what is the role of the mother in all of this?

THE DIFFICULTY OF BEING

As a rule, children with one or more alcoholic parents differ markedly from those whose parents are not alcoholic. They tend to suffer significant problems in defining their own identity and in determining what is expected of them. They often have low self-esteem and a poor sense of self-worth. They experience more problems socially and academically than children of nonalcoholics, and they are prone to drastic mood swings, frequently plummeting into those nether emotions known as anger, despair, and depression.

Researchers have also reported on the long-term consequences of growing up in an alcoholic home. Adult children of alcoholics, or ACOAs, experience considerable difficulty in areas of employment and marriage—even greater than individuals who grew up in similarly troubled families but without the specter of alcoholism. ACOAs often have problems parenting their own children, trusting other people, and forming and maintaining close or intimate relationships with others.

It has also been found that ACOAs are a greater risk in becoming alcoholic themselves and that if they do become alcoholic they tend to experience substantially more serious problems than do alcoholics whose parents did not abuse alcohol.

THE CHILD'S WORLD

The very nature of alcoholism makes it virtually impossible to provide children with an environment that feels safe and supportive. It is difficult for children to feel loved, cared for, and understood in a home where tension, anxiety, and chaos are the emotional furnishings.

For children, home is a reflection of the world—it is the world in microcosm—and for children of alcoholics home is often a very sad, lonely, and scary place. They do not understand what alcoholism is (who does?), and they do not relate to it as a disease—unless this fact is carefully explained to them.

What children *do* see—albeit somewhat simplistically—is that a father's abusive drinking and occasional abstinence is something that is in his power to control. Thus, when he consistently chooses to drink, the children feel rejected, unloved, and confused. They gradually realize—just like their mother—that they come second to the bottle, but they do not understand why. In their minds, Father knows how much his drinking is hurting them, how much it scares them, so when he persists in drinking, they see it as a sign of his not caring or as punishment.

Many children conclude that *they* must be to blame—maybe if they were better kids, quieter, smarter, nicer, more athletic, more successful at school, then maybe Father would love them more and would drink less. Sometimes this distorted perception is inadvertently reinforced by their nonalcoholic mother. When she tells them to play quietly and not to disturb their father, or when he himself becomes irascible about the children's behavior, she may send them outside or to their room, saying, "Now see what you've done—you've really upset your father."

The real issue, of course, is that Father is drunk; the children, however, are made to feel that his anger is caused by them. It was not necessarily the mother's intention to blame the children or make them feel guilty, but rather to prevent a bad situation from becoming worse: She knows what her husband can be like when he is drinking. But to the children the message appears to be that the problems at home are due not to Father or Mother or alcohol but to themselves.

These children are often left virtually without parents—in a sense, they are like orphans and maybe even worse off than orphans. While children who have lost their parents are generally identified and recognized as needing support and help, and efforts are made to provide them with the physical and emotional needs necessary for survival, children of alcoholics are much of the time ignored. They are seen as having parents, and although what goes on behind the walls of their home may be tragic, that tragedy is not easily visible to outsiders and is further camouflaged by the family's efforts to hide their shame, mask their unhappiness—and, motto of mottos, not betray the alcoholic.

A great portion of the alcoholic's time is occupied with that single, seemingly tireless theme of getting drunk, being drunk, and sobering up from a drunk. In the meantime the nonalcoholic parent is preoccupied with the consequences of all of this. We have already discussed the measures a wife will adopt to protect her family—tactics ranging from lying to the boss to pleading with creditors to telling friends and relatives that everything is fine so as to avoid embarrassment. By the time Mother has taken care of all these problems and provided as best she can for the physical needs of her children—cooking meals, dressing them, getting them off to school—she has just about exhausted all her energy. Attention to the more subtle needs of her children is virtually impossible. How much time and patience are left to play with the children? To read them stories, listen to their countless tales, answer their numerous questions? To deal with their feelings and give them advice?

The children hear their mother telling the boss that their father is sick, then shouting at her husband for being drunk. Chances are they do not understand that Mother is lying to protect Father's job. Similarly, they do not understand that she may be acting with the best, though perhaps not the most effective, of intentions. Instead they are left confused—and they often conclude that to tell anyone that their father drinks too much is not allowed. If Mother lies to others about it, then they had better lie too.

THE ABSENCE OF LIMITS

Feeling unloved, rejected, and to blame are by no means the only effects experienced by children growing up in an alcoholic home. In some cases children have to contend with physical violence against them, against their mother, or against both. In other cases they have to contend with sexual abuse. Though violence and sexual abuse are far from standard features of alcoholic families, they are certainly much more prevalent than in other families.

Even if they are not physically battered, however, children can be profoundly affected when they observe physical abuse between their parents and feel powerless to stop the horror. Many children who are witness to such terrifying events grow up with deep emotional scars that affect and influence all their interpersonal relationships.

Children need limits and structure. This is one of the main ways they learn the difference between right and wrong, acceptable and unacceptable behavior. When their boundaries are well defined, children feel reassured and secure. They will, of course, invariably test these limits—cross the street without permission, for example, or refuse to go to bed at the agreed-upon time—and a judicious parent will respond by disciplining in a fair and consistent manner. In this way children discover that the boundaries are not just haphazard whims but essential rules of the family, and that following the rules is important. This serves to reassure the children further, showing them that someone cares about who they are and how they behave.

When alcoholism invades the family, however, limit-setting becomes very difficult. The alcoholic himself is a prime example of limit-breaking. Clearly, if he drank within the limits, he would probably not be drunk. And because alcoholism cannot be controlled, the nonalcoholic mother may also find herself out of control. She may argue and even threaten separation or divorce, but the abusive drinking continues. Both parents thus become very poor models for limits themselves, with the end result that children become confused and unsure of what is expected of them.

As we have seen, when an alcoholic father drinks, he may become overly permissive with the children or he may become unreasonably strict. When he sobers up, he may feel remorseful and guilty for his previous night's behavior and grant the car without time limits and even throw in some extra spending money. On the other hand, while drinking, he may promise to take his son or daughter to the football game or the family on a picnic; but when next weekend comes around he is too drunk to do anything or has simply forgotten that he ever made such a promise. He is, in short, unpredictable, inconsistent, and untrustworthy.

In one of our early sessions, Melanie told of a typical incident with her father. Catching him in a good mood, she and her brothers pleaded to be taken to the circus. Somewhat uncharacteristically, he agreed to the request. They would go to the circus that afternoon, but first he had to withdraw money from the bank. The children, of course, were beside themselves. They listened confidently when their father told them to be ready when he got back from the bank, that he would be no more than thirty minutes at most. And they sat around the house, excited, their faces lit with anticipation, while the minutes ticked by. Thirty minutes became an hour, and one hour became two.

It was four days later when Father returned, bedraggled and sheepish and full of excuses and self-pity.

The circus by then had left town.

Children get hurt. They learn not to listen and not to trust. Most of all they teach themselves not to feel, because feeling is too painful.

DIFFERENCES AMONG CHILDREN OF ALCOHOLICS

Though it is often tempting to make generalizations about children of alcoholics, the truth is that—just like their mothers—they are not all affected in the same way. To talk about these children as if they were all the same is a little like talking about people who have been shot as all the same. While there is a certain element in common, someone shot in the leg is clearly very different from someone shot in the face or abdomen, and the treatment for one victim will be very different from the treatment required for another.

While some children appear to have been profoundly marked by the experience of living with alcoholism, many others seem much less affected, or affected in a different way, and still others appear no different from children raised in nonalcoholic homes. Why? There are various possibilities.

One is that parental alcoholism in itself is not the major cause for emotional and behavioral problems in the children. Numerous variables influence how children are affected and how they adjust, and indeed some of these factors are similar to the ones that account for the different effects experienced by wives of alcoholics.

The style and severity of the alcoholic's drinking, the degree of family disruption, the amount of physical and emotional neglect of the children, the presence or absence of siblings, the age of the children when alcoholism became a problem, the inner resources of the children, the children's relationship with their nonalcoholic mother, and the availability and accessibility of social support—all are variables that can to some extent determine how children perceive parental alcoholism, how they are affected by it, and how they respond.

SEVERITY, STYLE, BEHAVIOR

We have already seen that alcoholics vary not only in the amount and frequency of drinking but also in the severity of consequences. An alcoholic father may go on a week-long drunk every so often, while another drinks daily. One may drink at home, while another drinks outside and rarely gets home before the children are in bed. Some men are jocular, others belligerent, and still others are completely unpredictable when drunk—sentimental one moment, volcanic the next.

It is naive to imagine that a child who blushes at his father's drunken antics will be affected in the same way as one who is physically or sexually abused or who is forced to watch in frustrated impotence while a mother is being battered. This, of course, is not meant to suggest that children whose fathers are not violent are *not* affected. Quite the contrary, they may be very deeply affected—but not in the same way as someone exposed to constant threats or actual violence.

While one may feel ashamed and become more isolated, the other may become aggressive and as an adult may also be a spouse- or child-batterer. Though both may be able to benefit from psychological intervention, the kind of help each one needs is likely to be considerably different.

DEGREE OF FAMILY DISRUPTION

Often, life in an alcoholic home is a study in chaos, an existence disrupted by continual crisis and shaped by ongoing disappointment. Arguments arrive as spontaneously as tropical thunderstorms, unemployment looms constantly on the horizon, financial instability becomes a virtual watchword against which all ideas and actions are measured and chopped down to size. Confinement of the alcoholic in jail or hospital is not unusual. Separation and divorce and endless attempts at reconciliation are commonplace. So too are moving and changing schools.

On the other hand, in some alcoholic homes life appears to go on with hardly a ripple. Father's "delicate condition" is encoded—even absorbed—into the family organization, and though he drinks to excess, the actual level of disruption is held to a minimum. Everyone gets by, gingerly sidestepping the sore points that are inevitable with alcoholism, and perhaps content in the realization that things could be worse—that Father is a somewhat predictable and genial drunk who does manage to provide.

It seems reasonable to assume that the more disturbance and disruption caused by alcoholism, the more likely it is that the children will develop problems. Many clinicians report that younger children can be even more terrified by the arguments that go on between parents than by the actual drinking.

SIBLING SUPPORT

The level of chaos in some alcoholic homes is so extreme that even the most basic physical needs of children become compromised. Because Father is often drunk, Mother may be out working to help make ends meet, or she may be depressed and withdrawn or just plain exhausted and emotionally beaten, much like the stay-in-bed mother Melanie once described.

Youngsters may be left in the care of older brothers or sisters, or they may be expected to make their own meals, get themselves ready for school, and return home to an empty house after school—quintessential "latchkey kids." They may spend hours or entire evenings without adult supervision; they may miss meals, lack proper clothing or even reasonable hygiene. The consequences for these children in terms of loneliness, isolation, fear, and lack of love are very different from the consequences for children who do not endure this type and degree of neglect.

In a family in which there are siblings, younger children may receive encouragement and understanding from an older brother or sister, or the children may support one another by talking out their feelings together. The situation for an only child, however, may be altogether different, since he or she has no one to share with or lean on. If the parents are prone to violence or arguments, an only child may feel considerably more frightened and threatened than one who has siblings.

Though having brothers and sisters is no guarantee of supportive communication, there may still be a greater feeling of security in such circumstances, if only because of the sense of shared hardship. Nonetheless, the needs of one child may be much easier to provide for, and an only child may benefit in this regard. He or she may receive more care and attention, especially from a nonalcoholic mother, than would be possible if there were several children.

Though it is difficult to say which situation is more "advantageous," it seems reasonable to assume that the number of siblings can be an important factor in determining the effects of growing up in an alcoholic home.

AGE OF CHILDREN

Obviously, the needs of an infant are different from those of a young child or those of a preadolescent or teenager. Age also creates vast differences in a child's ability to understand and cope with parental alcoholism. While the two-year-old is dependent for all of his or her needs, the sixteen-year-old can take care of a great number of personal needs—not to mention having the ability to escape from the house and be with friends in periods of crisis.

Another important factor related to age is the time at which alcoholism becomes apparent. One child may be born into a situation in which alcoholism is already present, while another may have known his or her alcoholic father prior to the abusive drinking. In the first case the child has never known anything other than what is, while in the second instance the child can remember when circumstances at home were relatively good. He or she has to cope not only with the father's abusiveness but also with the memories of what it was once like *and* the loss of the father he or she once knew. This may at least partially explain why siblings often seem to have different views and impressions about their childhood experiences even though they grew up in the same home.

INNER RESOURCES

Children are not all born with the same inner resources. The way they are affected and the way they cope may be influenced as much by these inner resources as by external factors. It is difficult to determine why some children become overly responsible, while others appear rebellious and develop behavioral problems at home and school; or why some isolate themselves and seem to have no friends while others are rarely home and socialize a great deal. Some children turn into charmers and joiners; others become depressed and withdrawn.

The fact is, children of alcoholics grow up fast. They seek maturity as a moth seeks light. Many, in an effort to please the alcoholic parent, to survive the constant onslaught of outright criticism or self-inflicted blame, become perfectionists. This is one means of drawing away outside attention from the terribly imperfect situation at home. The tragedy is that perfectionists are all failures, are doomed to be such, because perfection is unattainable. As a result, like the ram that butts its head against the steel-and-concrete dam, they end up frustrated, conscious only of apparent inadequacy. As failures (who, in real terms, are actually successful) they often feel no better than their parents and thus turn to a familiar standby for solace and distraction. Is it really any wonder that such a high percentage of alcoholics come from alcoholic homes?

I once had to treat a young man named Steven. He was both alcoholic and the child of an alcoholic. He was tremendously successful in the stockbroking field, and despite the fact that he was drinking more and more he seemed to be reaping all the financial rewards that society bestows on a distinguished performer. In a sense, this seemed to endorse his conduct. Certainly, no one at the firm had spoken to him about his drinking—to some extent they seemed to regard it as a trapping, or eccentricity, of brilliance. But what went wrong? At a certain point he developed a terrible distaste for the money he was earning. He was squandering it—mostly on booze and barroom strangers—as though inspired by a death wish.

After some investigation we realized that while alcoholism was the primary problem, a secondary problem was guilt. His father had died drunk and bankrupt. According to Steven, when he was finally able to uncover the fact, it seemed somehow disloyal for him to better his father, to humble the memory of his father by becoming financially triumphant.

The point? That children of alcoholics, the perfectionists at any rate, find themselves in just such predicaments, find themselves confronting just such brick walls.

The "caretaker syndrome"—and we have glimpsed this in the case of Melanie—is just another facet of perfectionism among children of alcoholics. As I have mentioned, this is a role that generally falls to the oldest child in the family—the one who substitutes for an absentee or dysfunctional mother, the one who looks after the younger children, who picks up after everyone, who buys the groceries and cooks the meals, who tries endlessly to please and appease the alcoholic. Would it surprise anyone to know that the careers of many of these children— those who are female, at least—are unconsciously charted throughout their growing-up years? That a great number of them end up in professions such as nursing, being "caretakers," the area of occupation for which they seem naturally inclined?

What about the child at the other end of the spectrum? He is the one who does not seem very serious. Unless you scratch deeply, you will never have to wonder whether or not he got stuck in the caretaker role. The fact is, if you judge from his constant demeanor, he *seems* mildly irresponsible, somewhat oblivious to this terrible thing that is going on at home. He is the one who always has a quick and witty response, the one who can sometimes make you laugh in spite of yourself. It is true, his humor can at times seem a touch bitter, a touch cynical, a touch philosophical—a touch truthful—but it is after all humor, and humor is an inappropriate response to family difficulty. Or is it? Would it surprise anyone to know that a very famous comedian, a household name, was a child of an alcoholic? That he polished this escape mechanism, this survival strategy, to such a fine shine that the public at large flocks regularly just to hear him quip about life, its ups and downs?

Alcoholism is subtle—and its effects upon the shaping of our society are equally subtle.

Just as is the case with wives of alcoholics—and alcoholics themselves, for that matter—we do not know nearly enough about children of alcoholics. What we do know is that the previous examples are just some of the many coping mechanisms that children employ in an effort to adjust to parental alcoholism. It is the way they "choose" to adapt and survive in what is often a nightmarish environment. What we do not know is why some attempt to adjust in one manner while others use a different means. Is it a reflection of the many different factors we have talked about, or is it an indication of the innate resources of these children? Or maybe a combination of the two?

Equally important is the question of whether or not some of these coping strategies are more—or less—effective than others. Clearly, a great deal more research is needed to understand the effects of growing up in an alcoholic home.

ROLE OF THE NONALCOHOLIC MOTHER

Though family structure and parental roles have been undergoing considerable change in recent years, the primary caretaker is still usually the mother. Her inaccessibility because of preoccupation with her alcoholic mate and his drinking can be as detrimental to the children as their father's drinking.

On the other hand, her ability to detach from her husband's alcoholism in a healthy manner and to be more available for the emotional needs of her children is, in my opinion, a major factor in terms of filial stability. It is perhaps this, more than anything else, that differentiates those children most severely affected by the experience of growing up in an alcoholic home from those who appear to be much less or not at all affected.

Certain studies have examined the importance of the nonalcoholic mother-child relationship as a factor in determining the manner and degree to which children are affected by a father's alcoholism. According to Charles Deutsch in *Broken Bottles, Broken Dreams*, the apparent lack of emotional and behavioral problems in some children of alcoholics appears to be related to the nonalcoholic mother's "ability to maintain her own identity and get her own wants and needs satisfied, instead of reacting primarily to the alcoholic." Elsewhere it has been suggested that the quality of the emotional contact between a nonalcoholic mother and her children could lessen the negative consequences of growing up with an alcoholic father.

Certainly, my own personal clinical experience has consistently pointed to the nonalcoholic mother as potentially *the most important factor* in how her children experience parental alcoholism.

WHEN MOTHER PRETENDS

Children need at least one parent who is dependable, reliable, and consistent—the very antithesis of an active alcoholic. If a nonalcoholic mother becomes overly preoccupied with her alcoholic mate, the children are consequently left—like the orphans we previously mentioned—minus both parents. In this case, one parent is drinking and the other is busy trying to control and cope with the drinking. While the mother may feel that what she is doing is important for the survival of her family, she often becomes the object of their blame and anger, and is held responsible for everything that has gone wrong. She is the sober one—why has she not been able to do something to change the whole situation? We saw this in the previous "Voices," in the case of Jill. We also saw it in the response of Philip, Melanie's eldest child, to his mother's weeping.

Many women attempt to shield their children from alcoholism by pretending, telling their children that everything is fine or under control. A mother may try to keep up a good humor while falling apart inside. Children are not blind; they are sensitive to what goes on, and even though they may appear to be going along with a mother's pretense, chances are they know better.

The fact is, much of the problem in alcoholic homes is the anxiety and discomfort in talking openly about the situation. A great deal of the fear and confusion, however, can be alleviated with plain old-fashioned honesty. Certainly one needs to apply a little common sense and to take into account the child's maturity, but as soon as possible that child needs to be told that there is a problem, that alcoholism is a disease, that it is not his or her fault—he or she did not cause it and cannot change it—and that it is not something to be ashamed of. Children need to be encouraged to ask questions and to express their feelings. They need to know that talking it out is okay and that mother is there precisely for that reason: to listen to them and hear their concerns.

If you are a mother in such circumstances, share your *own* feelings with them—including your fears, worries, and concerns, as well as your hopes. Talk openly about the problem at home, and do not be afraid to use the words "alcoholic," and "alcoholism." Chances are you will be surprised. Not only will this tend to improve the overall atmosphere among family members, but it may encourage children— as we will discuss shortly—to feel more comfortable about seeking outside help and support.

Unfortunately, the foregoing is all somewhat easier said than done. Let us not forget that though the mother is a grown-up, she too is feeling confused, frightened, and concerned about what is going on—and quite unsure about what to do next. This is why external support—for her own self—is so important.

THE IMPORTANCE OF SUPPORT

If mothers—wives of alcoholics—seek advice and support, they go a good way toward overcoming much of their anguish. A woman who has received supportive counseling or has joined a group such as Al-Anon (see Chapter 10) is able to detach herself from her husband's drinking in a healthy way. As she begins to change her behavior and attitude, her children notice and tend to feel encouraged to do something for themselves too. Such a mother is in every sense a model for her children. In addition she is able to be more in tune with their emotional needs and to encourage candid discussion as well as involvement in groups such as Alateen or in sessions with school counselors. The end result is openness and a sense of security, rather than further isolation and shame.

Alateen is part of Al-Anon Family Groups. It is a self-help program for children, ages twelve to twenty, of alcoholics. The organization first started in 1957 and today embraces several thousand individual groups across the country. Each Alateen group has a sponsor, an individual who is a member of Al-Anon. Though the sponsor attends Alateen meetings, he or she does not ordinarily participate in the discussions but functions more in a guidance role and is available as needed.

In view of what we know about the potential impact that parental alcoholism can have on children, Alateen offers immense possibilities. Children need to know that they are not alone and are not to blame. They may feel ashamed of the alcoholic's behavior, worried that others will see what is going on, afraid that the alcoholic parent may accidentally get injured or killed—any of a host of emotions may course through a child's head where alcoholism is concerned. Alateen offers the children and adolescents an opportunity to work through a lot of this confusion.

When a child sees how other children live in similar situations and learns more about alcoholism, much of the shame and isolation is lifted. It is an extremely important beginning to the process of repairing the emotional damage caused by growing up with an alcoholic parent. But children and adolescents are resistant to going to such self-help groups. They are inhibited by their shame. They are afraid that going may further hurt or even anger the alcoholic parent, resulting in more drinking and arguing or even violence. Some feel guilty, seeing it as an act of betrayal because they are admitting to others that the father or mother is alcoholic.

One potential solution to this is, as we have noted, to introduce more open dialogue into the household. Nonetheless, children need to be encouraged to go, but not forced. Clearly, the best way of teaching is by the power of example—which is why a mother's own involvement in a self-help group is so important.

TRAPPED

It is very difficult to improve the lot of the child unless the lot of the mother is first improved. Both persons are integral, both prisoners of a very painful, grossly misunderstood drama. Yet, just as wives and mothers are labeled in the alcoholic universe, so too are the children—as codependent or paraalcoholic. There is a tendency to further stigmatize a group of people who have already suffered enough and who feel deeply trapped and isolated.

There is also, in our society, a propensity to be much more sympathetic to the suffering of the children than to the suffering of the nonalcoholic mother. Partly, this is human nature. Children are seen as innocent and powerless. Children of alcoholics did not choose their parents or choose to be born. They are not able to fend for themselves in any adult sense or to decide that enough is enough and leave—they are truly alcohostages.

The nonalcoholic mother does not receive such sympathy. She is an adult. She chose her mate and she can choose to leave him. But this, as we have seen earlier, is a terrible distortion of reality. These women are as trapped as their children, as unsure of what to do and how to do it. Many are themselves daughters of alcoholics. As children, they did not receive the help they needed and may have been deeply affected by the experience. Now they find themselves in a similar situation. When we help them—the Melanies of the world—we help the children. When we help the children we may, in the long run, make some inroad on the savage impact of alcoholism on our society.

MIKE'S "DRINK OR TWO"

The other "incident" that led up to Melanie's attempted suicide became painfully clear during that first joint session with her husband. As she explained it, Mike had come home in the evening clearly intoxicated. He wanted to take Melanie and the children to a local restaurant for supper.

Knowing that Mike was in no condition to drive, and that the restaurant was little more than an excuse for him to get even drunker, Melanie instantly opposed the idea, telling Mike that supper was already in the oven. A fierce squabble broke out, with Mike accusing Melanie of conspiring against him, of depriving him of the children's company.

As Mike became angrier, Melanie took refuge in the bedroom. Moments later she heard the front door slam and the car start. When she looked out the widow, she realized with horror that Mike had plucked the two children from the yard where they were playing and had taken them into the car with him. He had also, for some reason, taken the dog along.

Panicky, Melanie telephoned for a taxi and rushed across town to the restaurant. Predictably, Mike was already at a table, cocktail in hand. By now he was almost too woozy to grasp what was going on. Giving him no opportunity to react, Melanie snatched the children and fled back to the taxi.

AFTER THE RESTAURANT

As Melanie described all this, her face echoed the anguish she had felt that evening. Mike, crestfallen, merely listened in silence.

"But things didn't end there," she said. "That was just the beginning."

"Oh?" I glanced briefly at Mike, but there was no reaction.

"When he did finally come back," Melanie continued, "he was drunker than ever. And then . . ."

Suddenly her voice faltered, and she burst into tears. While she struggled to regain her composure, Mike broke in.

"What she's trying to say is that because of me the dog is dead. It's true, I was drunk—and I feel terrible about it—but it was still an accident that could have happened to anyone. On my way home I pulled off the highway for a minute, and the dog jumped out and ran in front of a car."

"And when he got home that night," said Melanie, her face still wet with tears, "he was like a madman, like someone insane . . ."

Half sobbing, she related how Mike had stormed into the house, accusing her of being responsible for the dog's death, for his drinking, for the children's unhappiness. The argument they had was far fiercer than any they had had before. Mike's yelling wakened the two boys. They arrived in the doorway just in time to see their father kick a glass coffee table clear across the living room.

As I listened to all this, I could not help wondering how long such a memory might remain entrenched in the children's minds. Forever?

Nor could I help thinking that because of alcohol, the man Melanie had long ago perceived as a Prince Charming was gradually turning—as she had said—into a Jekyll-and-Hyde. What was next, physical violence?

Dead dogs, smashed coffee tables. Children in tears over the loss of an old and faithful pet. A mother so depressed that she wanted to take her life. And all because of alcohol.

Because of alcohol, what once had been a love story was now beginning to resemble a horror story.

Key Points

• Unfair as it may seem, a wife's inaccessibility because of preoccupation with her alcoholic mate can be as detrimental to her children as his drinking. Outside help can be a major step toward overcoming this problem.

• Research indicates that younger children may be even more terrified by the arguments that go on between parents than by the actual drinking.

• Honesty is usually the best policy. If children are old enough to grasp the implications, it is wise to level with them about the parent's alcoholism. Explaining that it is a disease, that it is not their fault, and that they are not responsible will alleviate much of their confusion. Encouraging the children to attend Alateen (or to obtain some other form of counseling and support) is also of primary importance.

Voices: *Various children*

GROWING UP WITH ALCOHOLISM

• Janey, a nine-year-old daughter of an alcoholic father: "I know there is no God . . . because God could never let people hurt the way my mom and dad do."

• Pierre, a twenty-three-year-old son, both parents alcoholic: "When I look back, all I can see is two people rotting in booze and bitterness and obliviousness. It seems like a terrible waste, and it frightens me to know that that's where I come from. . . ."

• Suze, a twenty-five-year-old daughter of an alcoholic mother: "My biggest dilemma these days is children. Part of me wants to have them, the other part is afraid. I don't want them to grow up the way I did—and suppose I turn out like my mother?"

• Jake, a twenty-eight-year-old son of an alcoholic father: "I can't remember very much about my childhood, but what I do recall is how I used to cry myself to sleep—hoping and wishing that I might never wake up."

• Sandra, a thirty-year-old daughter of an alcoholic father: "I hated my father because he couldn't stop drinking and I hated my mother because she wouldn't stop yelling and crying. But I hated myself most of all because I didn't know how to help them."

• Cliff, a thirty-six-year-old son of an alcoholic father: "My father used to come in drunk and I would watch him stumble up the stairs. Sometimes he would head straight for the bathroom to puke his guts up, other times he would just stagger—and even crawl—into his bedroom. Most of the time he would make these pathetic attempts at getting undressed and then he'd fall onto the bed, usually with half his clothes still on. All the while my mother would be screaming at him, or crying, or helping him back off the bed and into the toilet. All of this used to happen right before my eyes—though I was usually crouched where no one could see me. At a certain point I just stopped watching, I was so disgusted and hurt; I could tell what was happening just by listening to the racket made by the two of them.

"One night my older sister began crying because of my parents' frequent fights. I guess she had just had it up to here. She stormed into her room and began smashing things and hurling objects against the wall. I think they were sculptures she had made at school and was—until that moment—enormously proud of. I remember her slamming the door shut and running into the closet to cry—as I myself had done many times before. She cried but she also tore down all the clothes, books, and other assorted junk that had collected there over the years. Finally she fell to her knees, screaming until she was completely out of breath. Then she just sat there sobbing.

"My parents finally heard Carol's wailing and came to see what was wrong. At first my mother tried to comfort her, but Carol told her to get away. She kept whimpering about how she just couldn't take it anymore, how she was losing her mind. 'I'm going crazy!' she screamed over and over again. All through this my mother kept hugging her and saying it's going to be better, it won't happen anymore. What a lie! It happened many, many more times.

"I was only nine years old then, but I'll never forget that night—and the hundreds of other hellish nights just like it."

• Jody, a forty-five-year-old son of an alcoholic father: "Once, after my father came home drunk for the thousandth time, I felt so angry, so frustrated, that when he asked me how my day was, I swore at him and spat in his face. He wiped the spittle off slowly and in a very sad and lonely voice, said, 'I'm sorry.' His eyes were brimming with tears

"I felt so confused, I wanted to throw my arms around him and say, 'No—I'm the one who's sorry. I had no right to do this!'

"I could hear a voice inside my head saying, 'Dad, I love you so much, I care about you so much—what are you doing to yourself, what are you doing to all of us? Please, please stop.' But words never came out. Instead I went to my room and cried and imagined how nice it would be to be dead.

"I guess I was ten years old.

"Today I am forty-five, married, and have children of my own. My eldest turned ten last week. After a beautiful birthday party and a day filled with fun and laughter, I tucked Jesse into bed. He put his arms around me and squeezed real tight, and said, 'Daddy, I love you so much.' I kissed him and held him tight for a moment until he asked me why I was crying. 'Because I'm so happy and love you very much, Jesse,' I whispered.

"When I came out, my wife asked if anything was wrong. I smiled and said, "No, nothing at all—I was just remembering a very sad, lonely little ten-year-old boy I once knew. . . .' "

Eight

Getting the Drinker to Stop

Drunkenness is temporary suicide

—Bertrand Russell

Mike had decided that therapy was not for him. He felt that his drinking was not the cardinal issue in the relationship, and that if Melanie would just "get herself together," he could handle his end of the situation—as he always had, he claimed. Though there was a great deal of discussion about all of these points, Mike was adamant. The one concession he would make was that he would stop drinking—not with the help of any program, but simply on his own, using willpower.

It seemed clear that Mike was still minimizing the severity of his problem and denying his dependence on alcohol. I had seen enough over the years to know that although willpower can certainly help an alcoholic stop drinking, it is rarely enough to keep him sober for very long. But I knew that I had to respect his decision; for now, at least, we would try things his way. Time would be the revealing factor.

My immediate concern was to continue working with Melanie. The objective was to help her increase her confidence and self-esteem while strengthening her ability to meet more of her own emotional needs. She had been making steady progress over the weeks, until one afternoon when she arrived uncharacteristically late, looking

145

extremely distraught. When I asked what was the matter, she hesitated momentarily, as though debating whether or not to tell me.

"I guess he's back to his old tricks again," she remarked.

"Tricks?"

"You know what I mean," she said, her anger obvious. "He's drinking—after all the promises and sweet-talking and all."

Melanie paused and took a deep breath, as though to calm herself.

"He got drunk on Friday, and I got so furious I told him to go to hell. Then on Saturday I refused to go to a dinner party with him, so the bastard went out alone and got drunk again. No apology, no nothing," she snapped. "I guess we're back to square one."

Melanie continued to speak about Mike's latest round with the bottle. If anything, she claimed, his drinking had become even more severe after his brief abstinence. Also, his potential for violence seemed to be on the rise. On the Saturday evening he had waved his fist in her face and had threatened to hit her—something he had never done before.

"What do you intend to do?" I asked.

"Well, I know what I'm *not* going to do—I'm not going to kill myself, he's not worth it. I know I should leave him, or at least get him to leave, but I just can't face that. I don't think I'm ready for that yet."

"Have you considered trying an intervention?" I questioned.

She looked at me, puzzled.

"What's that?" she asked.

INTERVENTION

An intervention is the bringing together of a group of people who are all very closely or intimately involved with an alcoholic. The purpose is to confront him in a firm but supportive manner about the reality of his situation, and to leave him with no alternative but to take appropriate, direct, and immediate action—such as entering a rehabilitation program.

Intervention is a very delicate undertaking and is not always advisable. As a rule, it should not be attempted without the help of a professional, because it requires skill and coordination. The people who should be involved in an intervention are those who know the alcoholic well, know about his drinking problem, and care about him and what is happening to him. They should be people the alcoholic loves, respects, or admires—in other words, people who would have influence on him.

When is an intervention desirable? It depends largely on the circumstances at home. If you are living with an alcoholic, you may have tried just about everything to pry him away from the bottle—everything from reasoning and pleading to arguing and threatening separation and divorce—yet this has not proved effective. You may have come to the realization that there is nothing you can do to force the alcoholic to change his ways. As a result, you may feel frustrated and bitter and afraid of what is happening to your life, yet worried and concerned about what he is doing to his. You do not know if you can put up with this any longer, but you also do not feel ready to leave. Intervention may therefore be the solution—it provides an opportunity to help yourself, and possibly, at the same time, to help him.

While the immediate reaction of the alcoholic may be negative, this is likely to be short-lived. Even so, you are not performing an intervention for the sake of thanks or appreciation—you are doing it for yourself, your family, and most certainly for the alcoholic. If it works, you have gained the world; if it fails, you have not really lost anything, but you now at least have the comfort of knowing that you have done everything you could.

SETTING UP AN INTERVENTION

The first step toward intervention is to engage the services of someone who is already familiar with the process. Not only does this bring expertise to the project, it also instills an element of objectivity,, which is important. An alcoholism specialist—a counselor or a therapist—is probably your best choice, though certain members of the clergy are also experienced in intervention.

The specialist will set up an interview with you in order to learn as much as possible about the alcoholic. He or she can also help you determine who should participate in the intervention. The list you arrive at should almost certainly include yourself and your children, if any, and possibly the alcoholic's parents and siblings, maybe a particularly close friend or coworker, and most probably his supervisor from work. The presence of a boss during intervention can be extremely helpful, since many alcoholics tend to hold up their jobs as proof that they do not have a drinking problem. A boss can usually dispel this falsehood by revealing how the alcoholic's performance really has suffered because of his drinking.

Generally speaking, five is an optimum number of people for an intervention session—this way the group is not so large as to be unwieldy (or overly intimidating to the alcoholic), nor so small as to run the risk of being ineffectual. An alcoholic in the throes of such an encounter may become very slippery and manipulative, so it is important that there be sufficient group pressure to counterbalance this behavior.

Many clients express hesitancy about involving young children in the intervention. They fear the ordeal will be too frightening for the children. My overall response is that it is a good idea to have the children participate. Aside from the fact that they probably already know that the problem exists and have already experienced at least as much fear simply as a result of the drinking, their innocent contribution can often be far more valuable than that of any adult. What is more, they have a right to their say—they need to be heard. In the process of sharing their own concerns, they will more than likely hear their insights echoed and seconded by the adults around them. This sense of support is beneficial. It lets them know that they are not alone, and that their perceptions are not askew. In other words, the experience can remove doubt and confusion.

Of course, if the children are unable to understand or speak, or if other factors come into play, then the youngsters should be excluded from participation. But again, the specialist will help you decide this.

SEEKING OUT SAMARITANS

After you have a list of potential participants in the intervention, the next step is to get in touch with them to determine their willingness to become involved. Not everyone may want to participate. Friends and coworkers may be worried about jeopardizing their relationship with the alcoholic. Children may be afraid of provoking anger. Parents may see their attendance as an act of betrayal. And there will be those who will feel uncomfortable simply because intervention is not a pleasant task—it is far easier to spend a night in front of the television and not think about the issue. If possible, get the individuals to meet with the specialist, so these misgivings can be discussed.

The specialist will lay out the facts clearly. Avoiding intervention is like driving past an accident victim on the highway—if something is not done immediately, the person may suffer serious disability or death. Though intervention may seem harsh, it is actually an act of mercy, a mission of kindness. In short, participating in intervention means that you care about the alcoholic, that you care about yourself.

PREPARING THE PLAN

Once the intervention team has been screened and identified, the next step is to have each member compile a list of incidents and observations related to the alcoholic's drinking. Not only must these be written down, they should be as specific as possible. Some examples:

• A wife: "Last Monday you came home at eleven o'clock at night. It took you almost two minutes to get your key in the door, and when you entered the bedroom you were staggering so badly you knocked over the lamp. You just fell on the bed and slept in your clothes."

• A daughter: "When my girlfriend came over two weeks ago, you were sprawled across the kitchen table, sleeping, and there was an empty bottle beside you. I was so embarrassed."

• A father: "Last week when you came to visit, you drove the car up onto the lawn and destroyed half my rose garden. When you saw my face you thought it was all very funny and began to laugh. Your breath smelled of alcohol."

• A friend: "You remember the last time we went out for lunch, about three months ago? You got so blitzed on wine that the waitress cut you off. Then you began to scream and curse at her, and everyone in the restaurant started staring. You know I go there regularly, so I was pretty upset."

FOLLOW-UP RESOURCES

So far, your plan is on track. You have your specialist and your team, and the lists are being prepared. One thing is missing, however. Assuming the intervention is successful, and the alcoholic acknowledges his problem and his need for help, what then? Where will he get the help?

The task now is to get in touch with whatever treatment or rehabilitation centers exist in your area. The specialist can doubtless offer a good deal of assistance in this regard. Other sources of information will be AA, local mental health clinics, and family service organizations. It will also be helpful to find out if the alcoholic's company has an employee assistance program to help employees deal with alcoholism.

When you have all the information at your disposal, discuss it with the specialist and choose whichever facility strikes you as most suitable. Find out about accommodation and availability, and keep this in mind when scheduling the intervention. Write down the address and, finally, the telephone number.

THE REHEARSAL

Now that you have a place for the alcoholic to go, you are almost ready to begin the intervention itself. However, since it is such a crucial and touch-and-go event, it is essential for the team to rehearse. A single rehearsal may be all that is necessary, but if there is any doubt, then a second or even third rehearsal should be considered. Whatever number of times you rehearse, though, keep in mind that the issue is urgent—the alcoholic needs help as soon as possible.

One of the first steps in the rehearsal is to decide on a chairperson. In this case it would probably be the specialist. Whoever is chosen, it will be this person's duty to direct the proceedings in an orderly manner and to monitor the various exchanges, ensuring that all the information is brought clearly to the alcoholic's attention and that emotions do not get out of hand. It is also the responsibility of the chairperson to make the opening statement, which should be simple and low-keyed and situate the alcoholic in the role of listener.

Here is an example of how the opening statement might be phrased: "Jack, everyone in this room has one thing in common—we care about you, which is why we are here. We want to help you, and so we'd like you to listen to what we have to say. It isn't easy for us, and it may not be very easy for you for the next little while. Even so, we know you're worth it, and we think the point is worth it. So will you just give us a chance and listen carefully to what's on our minds?"

The specialist will not only help organize the intervention, he will also look after details such as who starts. He will rehearse with you until everyone knows precisely what he or she wants to say. You will not have to rely on memory for your comments, because you can read from your paper exactly what you have in mind.

During the rehearsal it is also helpful to have team members take turns playing the role of the alcoholic. As the role-player hears the various comments made by other members of the team, he or she should try to respond in the way the alcoholic might. In other words, should someone say, "You could barely walk when you came home two nights ago," the role-player might counter by saying, "It's true—I was tired out because I had been stuck in a bar with a boring client who kept ordering round after round. I wanted to walk out hours earlier, but I couldn't without insulting him. It's not my fault I work in PR, you know."

Although it is unlikely that the role-player will anticipate the alcoholic's reactions exactly, his or her responses will help the team develop a sense of how the real intervention may go. It will give them a chance to prepare for various eventualities. What if the alcoholic decides to walk out of the room? Someone must be ready to say, "Jack, please sit back down and listen. What we have to say is important, and we're saying it out of concern for you." What if the alcoholic simply refuses to go for treatment? Then it may be up to the wife to present an ultimatum: "If you refuse to do something about your drinking, then I just cannot live with you any more—it has become that bad. All I'm asking is that you make the effort for all our sakes."

It should also be underscored that such responses—threats of leaving by a wife, threats of suspension by a supervisor—should be sincere. The alcoholic needs to realize that for once no one is bluffing. This is the end of the road. If he does not do something, his wife really will leave him, his supervisor really will suspend him. If the participants are not prepared to follow through on these ultimatums, then it is better not to bring them up at all.

There must be an air of firmness in the room at all times—though this should be tempered with compassion. The best way to preface every comment is with a positive statement: "Jack, I have endless respect for your ability, but lately . . ." Comments should also be as nonjudgmental as possible. Try to stay away from fuzzy insights and opinions, and stick with facts. Be objective rather than subjective.

It is also advisable to avoid the words "alcoholic" or "alcoholism." Given the ambiguity surrounding these terms, the alcoholic may find some leeway in dismissing them: "It's true I like to drink, but I'm certainly not an alcoholic—I can stop anytime, and you've seen it."

By avoiding the label "alcoholism," you will avoid getting side-tracked into definitions and discussions of precisely what constitutes an alcoholic. All that really needs to be conveyed is that the alcoholic appears to be having a problem with drinking, and that this in turn is creating problems for others. There is concern about his health. For the benefit of himself, and all the others in the room, would he consent to getting help to determine whether there is indeed a problem and, if so, how severe it is?

THE REAL THING

The intervention itself should take place on neutral territory—not on the alcoholic's home turf, where he feels in control, but also not in a place that might arouse anxiety. The home of a friend might be a good setting. Whatever the location, it should be free of interruptions.

It is also wise to schedule the intervention for a time when you know the alcoholic will not be drunk—a morning, for example. If the alcoholic is still hungover, possibly remorseful, then this may be an added advantage.

One member of the team must be delegated to bring the alcoholic to the intervention. Doing so may take a little tact, for the team member should try to give a minimum of information about what is actually going on. On the other hand, misleading the alcoholic may simply create hostility.

Another member of the team should be prepared to get in touch with the treatment center as soon as the alcoholic—assuming he does—acknowledges that he is willing to accept treatment. This may also be the person who explains to the alcoholic what is implied by treatment.

Another member of the team—possibly the wife—will probably want to have the alcoholic's bags packed and placed in the trunk of the car. The benefit of instant departure is that the alcoholic will not have a chance to change his mind, to have one last drunk and rationalize himself back to the bottle.

By the time the alcoholic arrives, all details should have been taken care of, and each member of the team should be fully aware of his or her role. The specialist is there to coordinate and control the exchange. If the alcoholic expresses anger, it will be necessary to defuse it as gently and firmly as possible. If he shouts at one of the members, it should make no difference—the participant should continue reading his or her notes regardless. The team must conduct itself with clockwork precision. It is a one-shot situation, and the goal is to make the intervention work.

There is no way to predict how an intervention will turn out. While much depends on how the team functions and how well prepared it is, much also depends on the alcoholic himself. Some interventions are almost miraculous in their outcome. The alcoholic walks into the room, the members begin to deliver their information, and he cuts them short. "You want me to get help, is that what you're saying?" he asks. "Well, no problem—just tell me how."

In other cases, the alcoholic will press for a compromise. He will not enter a rehabilitation center, but he will go to AA. In such a case, it will be necessary to pin him to a commitment. Will he go tonight? Will he continue going? If he drops off, will he then consent to treatment?

In still other cases, the alcoholic might simply say that he will stop drinking on his own. At such times—if it is true—it will be necessary to remind the alcoholic that he has already tried this route before and that it did not work. On the other hand, if he has never tried before, then it should be pointed out that the odds of stopping and remaining stopped on one's own are extremely slim indeed. Some kind of formal help is essential.

The moment that everyone is waiting for, of course, is simply for the alcoholic to say, "Yes, I guess there may be a problem here—but what is it you want me to do?" This is when you pull out all the stops. You tell Jack that you would like him to go to such-and-such a center for three or four weeks. When he agrees, you say, "Great! We've got you a room, your bags are in the car, and the company has agreed to grant you a leave."

At this point the intervention is over.

MIKE'S INTERVENTION

We had decided to hold the intervention at my office. Melanie had asked Mike to join her for one brief afternoon session, since his presence was essential, and though he grumbled and expressed misgivings, he eventually consented.

His first reaction upon entering the room was one of stark surprise. His parents and children were there, and so was an employee assistance consultant from work. His surprise quickly changed to anger, however, and he demanded to know what was going on.

As arranged, I spoke first, explaining to Mike that all those present were here because they were concerned about him, because they valued him as a human being. "Your family loves you," I said. "And they are afraid that they are losing you."

The words had the desired effect, and Mike calmed down. He took a seat and listened while I explained a little more about the purpose of the gathering. It was clear that he felt uncomfortable, but his attitude seemed to be a sort of "What the heck—I'll just bluff them out." That was fine, I thought. The main thing was that he stay and listen.

It was then time for Melanie to begin. Glancing at her paper, she told Mike how much she loved him, what he used to be like, and how she used to look up to him and always know that she could count on him. He seemed wise, caring, kind, responsible. But in the last few years, this had changed. She pointed out instances when he had been angry and unpredictable, times he had humiliated her at parties with his belligerence, and how friends had commented and had begun to drift away.

Almost the moment she stopped speaking, the two boys began. They took turns, with one explaining how upset they became when arguments broke out between their parents, and the other stating how afraid they were when their father did not come home on time—they were worried that he might be in an accident. They were able to remember specific evenings and specific thoughts they had had, and I was very impressed by the clarity with which they spoke.

Then suddenly the younger boy began to sob, and this triggered an identical response in his brother. Through the tears, they tried to tell their father how much they loved him, but that they felt he no longer loved them and they did not know why.

At this moment the emotion in the room was so strong you could have struck it with a hammer. There was a silent sob inside every adult, but it was Mike who completely broke down. He left his chair, tears streaming down his face, and threw his arms around both boys, hugging them tight. He told them they were the most important thing in the world to him, that he loved them desperately. He begged them to forgive him.

Both boys responded in unison, "Please get help, Daddy. Please, for us and for Mommy." It was a plea that only the hardest of hearts could have resisted, and it was clear that Mike did not have such a heart. He crept back to his chair looking shaken and forlorn.

Even though everyone was sensitive to Mike's reaction, there was no let-up. His parents spoke next, each explaining how worried they had become, that they too had been noticing the change in him. He no longer visited them as often as in the past, his father remarked, and when he did come the first thing he would do was go to the liquor cabinet, then pour himself a drink, then another, right up until it was time to leave. Once again, the information was given in detail.

Mike's mother, while supplementing many of her husband's points, also said that they were both very worried, that they felt guilty because maybe the situation was somehow their fault, maybe they were not very good parents, and that they were terribly concerned about Melanie and the boys.

At this point, Mike wanted to respond. I reminded him that it was important for him to listen right now, that his turn would soon come. He nodded wearily and fell silent again.

The final speaker was the employee assistance consultant. He explained that Melanie had originally telephoned him anonymously, and when he reassured her that she could speak with complete confidentiality, they had met. He reminded Mike that he had been asked by his supervisor on two occasions to get in touch with the employee assistance office, and that he had failed to do this. He also remarked that the supervisor had spoken to Mike several times about how concerned he was. The supervisor, in fact, had even contacted the employee assistance office to ask what could be done, short of disciplinary action.

According to the supervisor, Mike had been one of his best employees, but something had changed. His attitude was not the same, nor was his attention to detail. He had recently botched up an extremely important project, and had smelled of alcohol on several occasions in the morning. In short, unless there was a dramatic improvement, Mike was perilously close to being suspended.

As the employee assistance consultant concluded his comments, Mike remained speechless for several long seconds. He sat with his head in his hands, staring at the floor, then began to say how he had not realized how bad things had become, and how much he had hurt the people he loved. He certainly had not realized what he was doing to himself. He apologized to Melanie for having driven her to take an overdose, and explained that until this moment he had never really felt it was due to him. He had assumed that she was just an unhappy person and that she needed help.

Interestingly, Melanie responded by saying that she had once felt that he had driven her to this, but that she now understood it was not anybody's fault, that she simply had herself to blame for the way she had dealt with the problem. Now she knew better, knew that she could take care of herself, knew that she was not bad and not a failure—and that nothing could make her behave that way again, because she was now ready to face up to her problems. She felt confident about who she was, and only wished that Mike could feel the same way about himself.

I was impressed. Melanie had really come a long way in a fairly short time. I informed Mike about the need for entering a treatment center, and Mike hesitated. He wanted time to think about it. When I told him that arrangements had already been made, he complained that he could not possibly go right away because he was in the middle of a big project. At this point the employee assistance consultant spoke up, explaining that he had arranged for medical leave of absence, and that Mike need not worry about the job—his health was far more important.

The two boys asked again for their father to please say yes, to please get help, and Melanie—her eyes damp with emotion— seconded this request. Finally, Mike shook his head vigorously, as though to dislodge all awareness of his situation. He paused for a moment, then he spoke, his voice cracking: "Okay," he said "I'll give it a try."

Key Points

• When other methods of getting the alcoholic to stop drinking have failed, the technique known as intervention may prove to be effective. This means assembling a small group of key people from the alcoholic's life and confronting him—using prepared notes—about his drinking.

• The keys to a successful intervention are planning and rehearsal. Nothing should be left to chance; all details must be worked out carefully in advance.

• All members of the intervention team should conduct themselves with firmness, but also with understanding and compassion. It is essential for the alcoholic to know that they are there because they care.

• After the fact, many alcoholics express tremendous gratitude that they were a target of intervention. They are thankful that someone was concerned enough to go the extra distance.

Voices: *Jim, an alcoholic*

GOING THROUGH REHABILITATION

I didn't have to be pressured to accept treatment at a rehabilitation center; I decided on my own. I guess I was, as alcoholics often say, "sick of being sick." My drinking was bad, very bad. I had tried to stop countless times, but had managed only a day or two at most. Even AA somehow never clicked for me. I would go to a meeting halfheartedly, then afterward head off to a bar to wash the taste out. I hated myself for this. It seemed like one thing to fail as a human, but to fail even as an alcoholic struck me as ridiculous. Others were successfully getting sober—how come I couldn't? Was I somehow worse than other alcoholics? Was it perhaps that I was just not meant to be sober, that my destiny was to be a drunk forever?

Even when drinking I wrestled with these questions greatly, and it was this that finally made me get treatment at a center. It was like a last resort. As I arrived at the clinic, it all seemed so strange, so alien—in a way, it was as though I were going away to jail, and I might never see my wife, Joan, again. Realistically, I knew this was crazy—my stay would only be four or five weeks—but even so this was how I felt.

The nurse who interviewed me was pleasant enough, but rather sergeant-majorish. I later learned that this was deliberate, that the staff intentionally tried to take an assertive, no-nonsense attitude when dealing with the patients. By the time alcoholics arrive in rehab, most have long since lost all semblance of self-discipline.

Almost immediately after I was shown to my room, my bag was searched for booze, pills, and even aftershave. Apparently patients, out of desperation, have been known to drink the stuff—though, for myself, that was one of the few "beverages" I hadn't yet gotten around to trying. Afterward I was introduced to the other residents, an important part of the program being to get us to communicate without benefit of drink.

A typical day began with seven-o'clock wake-up. I had half an hour to get dressed, then clean up my room before breakfast. The attention to detail was very armylike. The beds had to be made a certain way, with no ripples in the blanket. The faucet and mirror had to be shining, without any fingerprints. The floor had to be mopped and the entire room dusted.

Breakfast—and all the other meals—was surprisingly good. This, I guess, was essential, because alcoholics tend to be prone to malnutrition—we substitute alcohol for food. Because of this, the meal was supplemented with vitamin pills. I had been drinking so long my body probably didn't even recognize the first few pills.

After breakfast there was room inspection, when two of the patients were charged with checking for tidiness. While they were doing this, the rest of us were assigned to various chores, ranging from vacuuming the carpets to dusting the hallways to cleaning the washrooms to doing the breakfast dishes.

At nine-o'clock prompt there was a general meeting in the main hall, and the room inspectors would read from their checklist who had done a good job and who had not. Points were won or lost according to the quality of the job, and although there was no real penalty, it became a source of competition among most of us to get a perfect score. The more times you got a perfect score, the more chance you stood of being made an inspector, which was sort of like being appointed a leader. Though it struck me as trite and thoroughly out of character, I actually found myself caught up in the rigmarole anyway. Truth? Well, I guess I kind of enjoyed it. . . .

At nine-thirty there was exercise outside, then at ten-thirty the first group session would begin. Sometimes this would be straight therapy; other times it would be a film on alcoholism, or a lecture.

Lunch was at noon. Afterward there was a forty-five-minute period of free time, then more group therapy. Some of these sessions were extremely tough, because there was a deliberate attempt to break us down, to get through our denial. I saw many tears, and a lot of anger. One buy broke a chair in sheer frustration. Another person—a young woman—tried to walk out of the room, but stopped when she was told that if she left the group she would have to leave the clinic. The therapy sessions usually lasted a couple of hours, then there was occasional one-on-one therapy before supper.

The evenings were free time when we were encouraged to talk, or get involved in games of cards or Ping-Pong or darts. It's ironic—you forget how to do a lot of these things when you're alcoholic, you forget how to play and have fun. The free time lasted until ten-thirty, then the group assembled once again in the main hall for relaxation exercises before bed. Lights out was at eleven.

For the first week of my stay I was not allowed any visitors or phone calls, the idea being to isolate me from the outside world and get me to concentrate on my problem, my alcoholism. I felt terribly alone during this week. I missed my wife like crazy, felt guilty about all the things I had put her through.

The second week I was allowed to make phone calls, but still no visitors. My first call was strange. I was so glad to hear Joan's voice; it felt like months since I had seen her. I was very nervous, sure she no longer loved me or wanted me. I told her how sorry I was for the things I had done, and she seemed a little surprised by this. I quickly figured it out—it had been years since I had expressed any feelings of guilt or sorrow toward her. I had been pretty well oblivious to what my behavior had been doing to her.

Joan was able to visit me on the third weekend, and I think what she found was a somewhat changed man. I felt very vulnerable, and was very quiet and soft-spoken. I guess I felt afraid of losing her, as though she might disappear from my life before I got out of the clinic.

The fourth weekend, I was allowed home. I had been given Antabuse—a pill that induces convulsions if alcohol is consumed—and warned to stay away from bars. I was also required to attend at least one AA meeting that weekend, under threat of expulsion if I cheated. I went along to the AA meeting that Sunday morning. It was actually the fourth time I had been to a meeting since entering the clinic, because AA held weekly meetings there which we were all required to attend. It was at one of these meetings that I stood in front of the group and read the twelve steps out loud for the first time, the twelve principles for getting and staying sober.

The weekend was passable. In a sense, we were like strangers. I'm sure it was odd for Joan to see me sober after all the years. And as for me, I felt almost afraid of her, almost like a child who is expecting to be punished. There was no question of our making love that weekend, though I desperately wanted warmth and affection. But I knew Joan was still too full of mixed-up feelings. So we slept together, took some long walks, and went out for supper a couple of times. We also talked a lot that weekend, and the conversation, though a little awkward and tentative, was also very sensitive. I did notice one thing about myself that struck me as very uncharacteristic. I had started to tidy up after myself, including cleaning the bathroom faucets and mirror—the training had evidently had an effect.

I went back on Sunday night, and the following weekend I was discharged for good. I came home armed with instructions. I had to attend weekly follow-up sessions with the clinic for the next thirteen weeks, and I also had to attend at least three AA meetings a week. Somehow, though, I felt that AA was working this time, that it was clicking for me. I guess the real point is that AA had not changed, it was me—my attitude—that had changed.

Did the treatment center work? Yes—it's been several years now that I have been without a drink, and my life has changed completely. The first part of that change came from the clinic. I cannot say the beginning was easy; it wasn't. I went through periods of frustration when I didn't know what to do with my emotions. It was as if I would suddenly have an intense feeling but nowhere to put it. In the past I had displaced these feelings by drinking. Now I had to find another way—and AA helped me in that.

Somehow, despite the initial hardships, I got through it, and I'm thankful that I did. My life with Joan now is better than ever. It's true we still have problems, like any couple, but somehow they don't seem so bad now that they're not magnified by alcoholism. I shall always be grateful to her for sticking by me, and I shall always be grateful that a treatment center was available for me, that the staff—though at times they were tough—cared enough and knew enough to be able to break me down and get me to face reality If not, I believe I would no longer be around to tell the tale

Nine ▃▃▃▃▃▃▃▃▃▃▃▃▃

If He Stops Drinking . . .

The worst thing about some men is that when they
are not drunk they are sober.

—W. B. Yeats

Well, he has finally stopped drinking and you are not quite sure how
to deal with it, or even how you feel about it. This may be the first
time he has tried to sober up, or it may be the fifth or fiftieth time.
Is this the real thing? Or is it just another break, a holiday away from
the bottle? How serious is he? Can he be trusted, or are you going to
end up hurt once more? Do you dare let yourself hope, dream, even
love again? What about anger? Can you tell him how much you have
suffered, what he has done to you, the children? Can you tell him
about all the silent tears you have shed, the nightmares and whirlpools? Or will this make him resentful—and worse, will it make him
drink again?

NOT "HAPPY HOUR"

These are just some of the many questions that wives of alcoholics are
tormented by, especially during the early stages of a husband's
abstinence. This period, the threshold of recovery, though not
recovery itself, might be called the *cessation* phase. Contrary to what

one might expect, it is not necessarily a time of joy and exhilaration; it is not "Happy Hour." For the family, and particularly for the wife, it can be a time of tension and anxiety. No matter how desperately a woman may have desired her husband's sobriety, the newly rekindled hope for a "normal" life is tempered by feelings of anger, shame, and humiliation, as well as by a fear that the alcoholic's resolve may not last.

Caught in this impasse, a wife has no way of knowing if it is safe to reinvest her feelings in a relationship from which, emotionally, she may have detached herself long ago. As a result, many women begin to mount various defenses, and attitudes such as skepticism, coldness, and indifference may be common. Though apparently directed at the husband, these feelings are more properly a reflection of her need to protect herself and her children from the painful possibility that drinking may resume.

During one therapy session, some weeks after Mike had successfully completed his treatment, Melanie expressed concern about some of her reactions. She was feeling anxious and unable to sleep, and her appetite had become meager. As well, Mike had complained about her aloofness and lack of humor. She commented that she was feeling puzzled and somewhat guilty about her behavior.

Given the circumstances, Melanie's condition was not as unusual as it may have seemed. The anxiety and fear associated with cessation can precipitate a recurrence or even intensification of the same psychosomatic symptoms experienced while drinking was still going on. Headaches, gastrointestinal difficulties, sleep disorders, and even depression are just a few of the discomforts that may crop up during this period. Fortunately, with time or therapy most of these difficulties disappear. The danger, however, is that many wives of alcoholics tend to seek medication as a means of reducing anxiety, and physicians can sometimes be cavalier with their prescriptions. It has, in fact, been suggested that twice as many women as men receive prescription drugs—and wives of alcoholics fall well within this pale. There is a tendency to overmedicate them, which unfortunately is often just one more way of not confronting the real issue.

Although the use of pills as a means of dealing with the various stresses of life may result in some immediate relief, they are not long-term solutions—indeed, they often create long-term problems. Even minor tranquilizers can become habit-forming, resulting in psychological and physical dependence. In some cases people experience various side effects, such as insomnia, headaches, agitation, aggression, and rage—in other words, the very symptoms they are supposed to be curing.

While some wives drink in response to a mate's alcoholism and others take pills, some take both pills and alcohol. Such a combination can be dangerous and sometimes lethal. And even if death is not a factor, stopping medications after prolonged use may cause withdrawal, which can be extremely harrowing and painful. Cessation after lengthy use of tranquilizers may result in tremors, abdominal cramps, sweating, nervousness, and intense confusion.

Even when medication is seen as appropriate, and prescribed by a licensed physician, precautions should be taken. First, it should be ascertained how necessary the drug really is, and what the level of dosage implies. Is it too strong? It is also important to ask the doctor about potential side effects, about possible interaction with food, drink, and other medication one might be taking, and about the length of time for which the drug is to be prescribed. Does it seem too long?

There are alternatives to pill-taking, which should be considered carefully and discussed with the doctor. It may be that a better approach to the stress lies in taking relaxation exercises, in talking over problems with a trusted confidant, in changing one's routine and activities—any of various possibilities may be far more beneficial than running the risk of becoming dependent on chemical solutions.

OLD PROBLEMS, NEW FACES

Because of her anxiety, Melanie had initially wanted me to arrange medication for her. After discussion, however, she decided to rethink her request. She then voiced another concern, related to an overall sense of disappointment. She had vaguely assumed that Mike's abstinence would somehow restore warmth and harmony to their relationship. Her disenchantment was based on a misconception that is surprisingly common among recovering alcoholics and their spouses: that once the bottles are gone, the marriage is automatically transformed into a joyous relationship.

Let us think about this for a moment. Many of the difficulties that were provoked by alcohol abuse—loss of employment, accumulation of debts, separation from friends, deterioration of health—may continue long after the actual drinking has stopped. These ongoing problems stand not only as testimony to a stormy past but also as a continuing source of stress.

As well, marital conflicts that existed before the onset of serious drinking—and independent of it—are often overshadowed by the family's preoccupation with the drinker and the inevitable crises that his drinking creates. Cessation brings these previously unresolved conflicts to the surface once again. A man who did not like to socialize before drinking, for example, is not likely to turn suddenly into a gregarious charmer now that he has stopped drinking. Similarly, couples who previously experienced problems in communication or sexual relations will require more than just sobriety to resolve these difficulties.

Most of all, however, cessation of drinking gives birth to a new set of issues and problems that can deeply affect the emotional stability of the wife and seriously imperil her alcoholic mate's efforts to remain abstinent. It is important to remember that just as active alcoholism has different consequences for different couples, so too does cessation of drinking.

Alcoholism, for one thing, does not develop overnight. It is a gradual process during which the wife reacts and attempts to adjust, as we have already seen, in numerous ways. Abstinence, on the other hand, is a sudden, practically instantaneous occurrence. The alcoholic stops drinking; ergo, he is abstinent. Unfortunately—and unfairly— the pressure is on the wife to adjust almost instantly. Therapists sometimes overlook this point, and hastily interpret the wife's lack of spontaneous support as a so-called negative response.

Some professionals, indeed, interpret the entire range of signals during cessation as evidence of the Disturbed Personality Hypothesis that we discussed in Chapter 2. The wife stays with the drinker throughout the years of active alcoholism—does not divorce him or even attempt to terminate the relationship—and then greets his abstinence with coldness and indifference. What is more, she may even deteriorate emotionally, becoming depressed and sick, *after* he stops drinking. Is this not proof of her complicity in his alcoholism? Unfortunately, to some specialists it is.

There is, however, another—and, I think, simpler—way of viewing this situation. Is it not a fact that the wife has survived a terrible emotional ordeal? There may be no broken bones or physical scars, but what about the invisible wounds caused by years of stress and mental abuse? While the alcoholic was drinking, the wife was expected to adjust and somehow make the best of a near-impossible situation; now that he has stopped she is expected to make a drastic change in course, to respond with warmth and enthusiasm and be fully, and *authentically*, supportive.

To see just how unrealistic such a demand is—instant turnaround after traumatic and possibly prolonged abuse—let us consider a familiar analogy.

THE WIFE AS RAPE VICTIM

Let us imagine for a moment that we are not talking about the wife of an alcoholic, but about a woman who has been raped. If she has no broken bones, no scars, no visible signs of having been in a struggle, should we conclude that the rape never happened, or that it was not quite as bad as she says, or that she did not resist? If she did not in fact resist, does this suggest that she did not mind being raped, or that she enjoyed or "needed" it?

Days or weeks after the ordeal, if she begins to feel depressed, is contemplating suicide, or is simply cold and indifferent to her mate and unwilling to have intimate relations with him, does this indicate that she has serious underlying problems that predispose her to a "need" to be raped? Should we presume that she simply cannot function in circumstances where rape is not occurring?

Not only are such conclusions ridiculous, they are also outrageous. Yet this is precisely what supporters of the Disturbed Personality Hypothesis would have us—and worse, wives themselves—believe about women married to alcoholics. Such conclusions have done irreparable harm to numberless women.

Why would a rape victim not resist? Presumably because she is paralyzed with fear, because she senses that her life is at risk if she struggles or attempts to escape. The survival instinct plays a similar role in women married to alcoholics. Though wives stay in the marriage for a variety of reasons, as we have seen, many remain because of fear of physical abuse, or death itself, if they even attempt to leave. Most of all, however, wives have tended to stay because they perceived no choice. As long as her alcoholic mate was still working and she and the children were economically dependent, they had shelter and food—leaving might jeopardize the survival of the family.

The emotional consequences of rape may continue long after the rapist has been arrested. His arrest does not undo the rape. Why then are we surprised when wives of alcoholics appear tense, apprehensive, emotionally distant, and depressed after their mates' alcoholism has been arrested? In reality, the threat is still there. So too are the scars, the memories, and the distrust.

Cessation is much like this. In many instances the wife emerges tremulous and wary, as though after a rape. What is more, it is only now—now that the alcoholic's drinking has been arrested—that she is able to take time for herself, to reflect on years of abuse, broken dreams, and wasted opportunities. Is she going to be upset? Of course. Is she going to be angry, hurt, moody, scared, sad, skeptical? Of course.

The preoccupation with daily crisis is over—what better time than now to fall apart?

WHY DID HE STOP?

But is that all? Is the wife's reaction the only factor that shapes this phase called cessation? The answer is no. And again, this is something that professionals sometimes overlook.

What are the reasons for stopping the drinking in the first place? If an alcoholic husband stops because of external circumstances— danger of job loss, threat of imprisonment, even a doctor's warning— the wife's reaction can be expected to be less enthusiastic and less supportive One need not look far to find the causes:

- He is not stopping because his drinking is affecting his family. He is not stopping in response to their pain and pleas. He is stopping because he is being forced to by external pressures. Very often such an alcoholic will continue to behave like a drunk even when he is not drinking.
- He is mourning the loss of his bottle, and is likely to be very hostile because he has been forced to stop.

Under such circumstances, an alcoholic's behavior and attitude may be so detestable that a wife might actually prefer him to be drinking again; realistically, he may be easier to coexist with.

But what about the alcoholic who stops for the "right" reasons—the one whose decision is made in response to internal factors? Here the alcoholic has determined for himself—possibly after discussions, even arguments, with his spouse—that the time has come to do something about his drinking. In such a case a wife's reaction will probably be quite different. She may be far more supportive and willing to risk emotional involvement. And the alcoholic's own reaction may also be different because he has made the decision for himself.

This kind of stopping is usually the basis for what is sometimes called "good sobriety." In all likelihood it may lead to what AA people refer to as serenity.

NEW RULES, NEW ROLES

As we have seen, a wife often out of necessity takes over numerous activities and responsibilities that were previously her husband's. Everything from being principal breadwinner to paying the bills to disciplining the children may gradually have become her sole domain. Now that the alcoholic has stopped drinking, however, he may try to make up for years of so-called absenteeism.

The husband may plunge into his new role with a seeming vengeance, a reaction perhaps to the recent rigors imposed upon himself. Maybe this will show itself in a sudden need to be uncharacteristically stern with the children, to instill new values. It is equally possible, however, that the effort will be gradual, even subtle.

Either way the wife may find it difficult to return control of certain household functions. Chances are, she now knows that she can handle these affairs successfully. Can she say the same for her husband? With what assuredness can she trust his judgment? And—the eternal question—what if he starts drinking again? The entire structure she has set up is likely to come tumbling down like a house of cards. She does not want to go through that twice!

What is more, a wife may resent her husband's sudden resumption of authority, especially if there is a lack of awareness of her sacrifices and efforts. While he was more or less mentally and emotionally (if not also physically) absent, she was struggling to run a one-woman show. Where is the acknowledgment?

The husband, for his own part, may expect his wife to receive him with warmth and enthusiasm. After all, he has done a good and difficult thing, giving up drinking. Regardless of his own feelings on the matter, it was also what *she* wanted for so long. Surely a reward of some kind is implied? He may expect a return to intimacy and sexual relations with her—but she is simply not ready for this. Not only is she afraid of letting herself feel and dream and hope again, she

may even be wrestling with various negative feelings ranging from
anger to deep sadness.

While she was coping with her husband's alcoholism, living in a
state of almost daily crisis, she had little time to focus on her own
needs and problems. Now that she finds herself liberated from this,
she begins to recall all the broken promises, missed opportunities,
the years of neglect, abuse, and shame. Part of her wants to confront
him with the facts, to be certain he knows and understands what she
has had to endure. When he was drinking, her begging, pleading,
arguing, and recrimination fell on deaf ears; he was simply too drunk
even to recall what had taken place.

Another part of her, however, wants to avoid any disagreement
with him now that he is sober, for fear that it may trigger a new round
of drinking. She feels bitter and hurt about years of victimization, and
fearful and concerned about appearing like a villain if she confronts
him. The end result is that once again she feels trapped—an
alcohostage caught between vague optimism about an unpredictable
future and unresolved anger about an unresolved past.

What makes matters worse is that friends—AA pals, if he is in the
program—and family members are expressing excitement about the
newly sober alcoholic and offering him their support and congratulations. Amid all these pats on the back, the wife may feel suddenly
redundant. Can it be that nobody recalls *her* ordeal in those
not-so-distant drinking days, that nobody is aware of *her* role in
"holding the family together"? Without her patience and effort this
day might never have come. Yes, it is his party, but she is the one
who "paid" for it and helped set it up. How come she is now the one
least acknowledged and least able to take part?

OFF ON A PINK CLOUD

The newly sober alcoholic is also going through numerous changes
both emotionally and physically. Yet not every alcoholic adjusts to
abstinence in the same way. Some go through a lengthy period of
mourning, literally grieving. The bottle was once their ally, their
most steadfast companion, their mistress, their everything. Now she
is gone, and presumably forever. Even if the decision to stop drinking
was his own, the alcoholic may feel a good deal of sadness and a sense
of utter loss. Such an alcoholic may be very difficult to live with,
especially in the early stages of adjustment. He may be very moody,
temperamental, and aggressive.

On the other hand, there is the alcoholic who appears to take to abstinence like a fish to water. He stops drinking and absolutely nothing appears to bother him. He is jovial, ebullient, relaxed, positive, and most of all very confident. He has hit the jackpot, and his only question is *why*—why did he not do this sooner? He is amazingly energetic, gung-ho about the smallest things, and he enjoys going to parties and does not appear to be the least affected by people drinking around him. In fact, he is mildly offended if they do not. Friends, colleagues, and even family cannot believe the change. Those who are not familiar with alcoholism sit back and admire this miraculous turnaround, this splendid metamorphosis. But those who are familiar with alcoholism—who recognize it for the cunning disease that it is—know that this man is in big trouble. Among AA folk, he is referred to as being on a "pink cloud."

This man is not recovering from alcoholism; he has merely escaped temporarily into a world of denial no less severe and no less dangerous and precarious than the denial that attended his drinking days. He has bypassed the painful journey of recovery by avoiding having to look at the real issues of his life. He has somehow convinced himself that all his problems were due to drinking—and now that he is not drinking anymore, his problems are clearly over. His perception is as disturbed as it was when he drank. True recovery is a process of growth, and it involves facing up to the many losses that were incurred during the days of oblivious drunkenness.

Once the pink cloud evaporates—as it surely will—the hapless alcoholic falls swiftly to earth, plummeting into despair and confusion. He feels let down, betrayed, and he may well seek to regain euphoria by drinking again.

CHILDREN'S PUZZLEMENT

Even when pink clouds are not the issue, however, a recovering alcoholic may still feel disappointed. The apparent coldness and indifference with which his wife responds to his abstinence may be seen as revenge, vindictiveness, and hostility. In the eyes of her children there is often puzzlement: They are not sure what to make of Mother's attitude. I recall eight-year-old David—the youngest son of Melanie and Mike—and his sense of confusion in this regard. It was during a consultation with both parents and the two children present. I had asked David how he felt things were going at home now that his dad had stopped drinking.

After a moment of silence and looking with big brown eyes at one parent, then at the other, he answered in a small and thoughtful voice:

"I sometimes get mad at Mom 'cause Dad tries real hard to make us all happy—and when he kisses her she doesn't kiss back, and she never smiles. But then sometimes I don't get mad 'cause I know that Dad used to make Mum cry a lot and I think she's afraid that he's gonna make her cry again—and so I'm not mad at her so much. . . ."

The small voice trailed off, and the large velvety eyes looked again from parent to parent, unsure whether he had said the "right" thing. There were tears in both Melanie's and Mike's eyes. His older brother looked down at his knees in stony silence. Suddenly both parents, one, then the other, hugged David and kissed him. I believe I had another question for this little fellow, but I lost it while blinking back my own tears. Family therapy, as we will see later, can be very powerful.

A DILEMMA

Compared to the way their home life had once been, the situation between Melanie and Mike had improved considerably. No longer was there any talk of lost dogs and smashed coffee tables, no longer was there the nightly ritual of waiting for Mike to stumble in drunk. He seemed to be embracing his newfound sobriety eagerly, and, much to his surprise, was even enjoying AA—he found the warmth and supportiveness of the members stimulating, and was going to three or four meetings a week.

Sometimes, during the first flush of sobriety, alcoholics may seem to overdose on meetings. Where a beginner is concerned, this may be a good and necessary thing. The alcoholic at this time tends to feel somewhat precarious about not drinking and needs all the support he can possibly get. More often than not, the people best able to provide that support are other alcoholics, individuals who have triumphed over the bottle and who, by their mere presence, are walking proof that it can indeed be done. The other side of the situation, however, is when an alcoholic continues this pattern on an indefinite basis, using meetings as a total substitute for drinking. Whereas before he was always in bars, now he is always at a meeting, and the wife may again feel neglected and resentful.

While I sensed that there was a certain element of concern that

Melanie and Mike were experiencing but not expressing, Mike's attendance at AA did not seem to be the cause. Even so, based on what their youngest son had said and on my overall impression, it was clear to me that something was bothering them. After young David had spoken, I probed the issue further.

Melanie said: "Speaking for myself, I feel very uncomfortable, as if something is missing. I mean, Mike has his AA, and he certainly seems to be gaining a lot out of the program. I have my Al-Anon and my therapy, and those have been fine—I actually don't know where I'd be without them. But even so, while we both have our own programs, we don't seem to have anything that can help us grow as a couple."

Mike interjected, "I guess what she's saying is that we've both been through a lot, and now it's like we're getting to know each other all over again—and it's not easy."

He thought for a moment, then continued: "Mel is right, you know. She goes to her program, I go to mine. I can't help thinking it would be far more beneficial if we were both enrolled in the same program—I don't mean me going to Al-Anon or her coming to AA, but something that we both have a joint investment in, something that is helping us both at the same time, something we can share."

"Well, maybe it's time you considered family therapy," I said. "I recommend it, particularly at this stage in your relationship. I feel certain it would help not only both of you, but also the two boys."

After explaining a little about family therapy, I gave them the names of several family therapists, while explaining that in view of the fact I had been Melanie's therapist for some time now, it would be inappropriate for me to see the whole family. It might interfere with her ongoing individual therapy.

After a brief discussion, everyone agreed to give family therapy a try. Mike himself was surprisingly positive.

"I think there's a lot at stake here," he commented. "I know that there are still lots of unresolved issues and I want us to get at them before they get at us."

The change in Mike was beginning to look truly impressive. He was a far cry from the bowed man in the chair the day of the intervention. Now he seemed to have pride and energy, a zest for life and a renewed sense of purpose. One got the feeling that he was ready to take on the world, if necessary, to make things as they once had been.

Key Points

• When a spouse stops drinking, the relationship does not automatically run smoothly. While problems created by alcoholism may still need to be resolved, various other underlying problems—which have nothing to do with alcoholism but which may have been overlooked because of alcoholism—may also need to be resolved.

• As a wife, your response to the alcoholic's abstinence may be less than enthusiastic. This is normal. Many of the fears and memories created by the past still have to be worked through.

• It took time for alcoholism to develop; it will take time for its impact to diminish and for trust to be reestablished.

Voices: Helen, a wife

THE QUALITY OF SOBRIETY

You may find it ironic: I broke up with my husband not because he drank but because he *stopped* drinking. Don't get me wrong—when he drank, I hated it. All I ever wanted was for him to stop, and I did everything I could think of to achieve this. I nagged, reasoned, pleaded, poured bottles down the sink, threatened to leave, tried drinking with him to limit his intake, asked friends of his to intervene, approached his family for help—nothing worked. Then one day out of the blue, he simply swore off. . . .

The way it came about is strange—at least, if you believe his version of it. One evening when he was driving home drunk, his car went off the highway and plunged down an embankment. Another few feet would have cost him his life. He emerged from the car nervous and shaky, scrambled back up the embankment, and then— so he claims—he heard a voice behind him. It was the voice of God, telling him to turn his life around.

Truth or not, the experience certainly had an effect. He came home that evening, telephoned AA, and as far as I know has never touched a drop since. That was at least seven years ago. At first, I have to admit, I was a little suspicious about whether or not the "cure" would take—I mean, nothing else had ever worked. But even so, it was a step in the right direction, and I was willing to hope.

The first year was simply terrible. He was out at AA meetings and with AA friends at least as much as he had been out when he was drinking. People from the organization told me not to worry, that the situation would eventually change and that the first year was critical to his sobriety. I accepted that, since I think in most cases it's probably true.

But the fact is, things didn't change. If I hadn't been a widow before, I was certainly a widow now—or at least the equivalent of one. On the rare occasions when my husband was home, he seemed remote and sullen and thoroughly untalkative. I began to think that I was guilty of some kind of crime, maybe the crime of *not* being alcoholic, of *not* being a member of AA (though I did go along to some meetings with him). There was also a lot of God-talk in the house, as though he alone knew who and what God was all about. I'm not an unbeliever, but the truth is, he was beginning to drive me crazy.

It was probably midway into his third year that I began to ask some serious questions. Where, I wondered, was the man I had married? We had first met at a dance, and he had been lively, witty, thoroughly engaging—the very opposite of what he was now, with me at least. Frankly, I felt cheated, deceived. I felt I had been sold a false image, a phony bill of goods. It was as though I had bought one personality, opened the bag when I got home, and found another—and no exchange was permitted. What a lousy trick, I thought.

Even when I questioned Colin about his changed attitude, there was this terrible sense of self-righteousness that came to his defense. "Which would you prefer?" he would ask. "That I start to drink again? We both have to accept certain compromises." Well, compromise was one thing, and though I admired Colin's efforts to stay sober, I felt that I had done more than my share—putting up with him when he was drinking, and stepping on myself when he was getting sober. Where was *my* life in all of this?

I guess we trudged on in this mess for several more months, until one day I learned—to my horror—that Colin had committed what is called in AA circles a "thirteenth step," a thing that is certainly not endorsed by the AA philosophy. In short, Colin was having an affair with a female member. I was disgusted, and I was hurt, and that was the day I left our marriage of twelve years. Fortunately, there were no children.

I don't know what to say in closing. Was I a great wife? Hardly. I'm sure there are things I could have done better, more attentively. But I'm convinced—without prejudice—that in principle I was as good as they come. I tried to keep Colin happy, I tried to be supportive. Love and understanding were always available. I honestly believe that Colin fell prey to what some AA members call "poor sobriety." Whatever they were offering was something he didn't fully get, the positive serenity they sometimes talk about. Whether Colin has got it now, I can't say—I haven't inquired. I'm busy with something more important. It's called my own life. And it's a good one.

Ten

The Road to Recovery

We are not on earth to see through people but to see
people through.

—George Eliot

We tend to think of recovery from alcoholism as the exclusive domain
of the person with the drinking problem. We often forget that
recovery is also an essential process for those who are intimately
involved with the alcoholic. These individuals—spouses and children,
as a rule—need to recover from the experience of living with
drunkenness.

Obviously, if an alcoholic is himself able to effect a successful
recovery, the domestic situation may be off to a promising start.
Nonetheless, some families may have to hold their breath for a very
long time before such an event takes place—if it ever does. More than
a few alcoholics drink themselves into the grave, leaving behind a
mess of scrambled memories for the family to sort out. Other
alcoholics simply drink until they are well on in years before choosing
to quit. Some alcoholics may enter recovery and then have what is
called a slip. That slip may last for days, weeks, or years—and it may
occur at any time.

The point? That a wife's recovery (and that of her children) should
be—in fact, has to be—independent of the alcoholic's performance.
Whether her partner is drunk or sober or somewhere in between, a

175

wife must begin to look at herself and identify some of her own needs. The time to start, of course, is as soon as possible

A LEGACY OF SCARS

For Carla, the immediate issue of living with an alcoholic had been drastically erased with the death of her husband. This, however, did not mean that the experience could simply be rolled up and put away. All human beings leave emotional legacies in their wake, and alcoholics are clearly no exception. Sometimes the legacy is the bittersweet remorse that Carla felt, the lingering love-hate impulses, the guilt and self-blame that were all too visible during her early days in therapy. Other times there is just pain, and the pain looks big and endless.

Emotional pain, though it may subside with time, can leave scars and wounds that continue to affect the way a person feels within and interacts with the world at large. Even if your partner has stopped drinking or is gone from your life, the consequences of having lived with alcoholism can continue to influence your attitudes, self-perception, and interpersonal relationships for years, possibly forever. What is needed is an opportunity to deal with the experience and come to terms with it once and for all. The question, though, is: *how?*

For starters, you need to talk about it, acknowledge what has happened and what you have been through, and let your anger, sadness, hurt, fears, and self-doubt come to the surface. Obviously, this takes courage and effort. Nonetheless, it is the best—if not the *only*—way of truly recovering from the ordeal of living with alcoholism.

You further need to recognize, understand, and accept that you are *not* the cause of your partner's drinking problem, no matter what he may claim. This, of course, may not be easy, especially in a society that has often reinforced the alcoholic's denial and projections by consistently seeking to establish links between his abusive drinking and the behavior, attitude, and general personality of his mate. Nonetheless, this should be primary in your mind, that you are not responsible.

A third step is to reject the concept of alcoholism as a family disease. Neither you nor your children are diseased, though you have doubtless been emotionally *affected*. Even so, this is far from being sick or mentally disturbed.

A fourth and tremendously significant step is to involve yourself in a self-help group, possibly in combination with a competent and caring therapist. Perhaps more than anything else, this can help heal the scars and gradually enable you to grow to your potential: to live and not just exist, to enjoy and not just be—in short, to experience life at its fullest.

RESTORING HAPPINESS

Despite the tragedy of her recent past, Carla seemed to be progressing steadily. With the help of therapy and participation in Al-Anon, she had started to recognize that she had not been responsible for Bob's drinking or for not being able to put an end to it. Certainly she had tried in her own way to do something about it, as any wife might, but the final decision lay with Bob.

Al-Anon had proved to be a particularly effective tonic. It had exposed her to warmth and friendship, and also the very real fact that there were other women who had been through experiences similar to her own, and they had survived. She saw happiness in some of these faces, and she saw hope for herself. She gained philosophy, and she gained a very important awareness that she was not alone and that the world was not as big and empty as she had initially perceived it during her grieving.

In spite of all this, Carla continued to feel a sense of concern about her relationship with her children. Though she couldn't put her finger on anything specific—they were polite, respectful, and mindful of her—they seemed rather cold and emotionally distant. She had tried talking to them about this, but they denied that anything was wrong. Carla could not help wondering whether they were holding her responsible for their father's death, or whether they had been affected by her depression following the tragedy. Whatever it was, Carla felt she needed help with the situation and wanted to know if I would see her and the boys together. I consented.

Though the children readily agreed to come in, they were somewhat reluctant to say much—they seemed shy and cautious. In retrospect, I can hardly blame them. I had gone about the whole matter rather clumsily. Instead of giving them an opportunity to get comfortable, I had probed a little too deeply and a little too quickly. Toward the end of the hour, I asked if we could all meet again the following week; I had a plan. The next session I showed them a film that focused primarily on an alcoholic father. Afterward, when I asked what their thoughts were, it seemed evident that the device had worked: The boys began to talk more freely and identified with the children in the film.

As we talked about their own feelings and experiences, they explained how often they had felt embarrassed and afraid to bring friends home, but that their biggest fear was the screaming and arguing between their parents. They clearly had many questions for Carla, and for me. A lot of feelings that had been stored inside were now being shared quite openly. There was pain and there was love but more importantly the doors of communication had begun to open.

One of the boys, the eldest, remarked to Carla: "I guess I've wanted to ask you things or tell you things about you and Dad, you know—but I was afraid it would make you cry, that you'd get all upset again—"

"Yeah," said his brother. "And then you'd take the pills again and start to drink like Dad did, and then we'd have to go to Grandma and Grandpa again—"

"Shut up," muttered the third boy, the youngest. "Don't say that."

From the conversation it was becoming clear that though there were a lot of issues, the primary one was *trust*. The children had lived through parental alcoholism, marital breakup, father's sudden death, and then simultaneous loss of their mother to pills and alcohol.

Carla's response was excellent. She instinctively knew that defending herself or making promises was not the solution. "This is why I go to therapy and Al-Anon meetings. It is to help me so that I never need to depend on pills or alcohol again. I love you very much and I know that with time you will be able to trust me again."

WHAT IS AL-ANON AND WHO IS IT FOR?

The organization that had been so effective in helping Carla came into existence in the early 1950s. The fellowship was founded in response to a growing recognition of the needs and problems of those who live with alcoholics, and today it is one of the most respected of all self-help groups. It offers information, education, and emotional support to spouses, children, relatives, and concerned friends of alcoholics.

Is there an Al-Anon group near you? Chances are, yes—there are now more than 25,000 groups around the world, and this number is increasing steadily, a clear indication that living with alcoholism, while it may seem to be an enormously individual problem, is far from unique.

Although Al-Anon is separate from AA, it models itself after AA and closely resembles that organization in structure, function, and vision. In other words, its philosophy is embodied in a simple twelve-step program—and, as many members will tell you, if you want it to, "it works."

At present, women—usually wives and female companions of alcoholic men—constitute the majority of Al-Anon members. My personal impression has been that many of these women are daughters of alcoholics. Regardless of their background, however, the female members differ in age, culture, and socioeconomic status and are involved in many types of relationships with alcoholics. Some are legally married; some are not. Some are living with their alcoholic partner; some are living apart. In many cases the partner is actively drinking, in other cases he is in the process of stopping, and in still other cases he has already stopped, months or even years earlier.

Do men attend these meetings? The answer is a limited yes. In recent years more and more husbands of alcoholic women seem to have been joining Al-Anon; unfortunately, however, they still remain underrepresented. It would appear that they continue to ignore the problem of a wife's alcoholism as long as possible, and when no longer able to do so tend to choose separation or divorce. This is just one more inequity that needs to be addressed.

Men and women who are adult children of alcoholics? Though formerly they would join Al-Anon, and some still do, they now have the option of involvement in a very fast-growing self-help network called ACOA—Adult Children of Alcoholics.

AL-ANON MEETINGS

Each Al-Anon group has regular weekly meetings. Many members, however, belong to more than one group and attend several meetings a week. Most meetings are held in the evening, but more and more are taking place in the morning and afternoon, seven days a week.

There are differences among groups, but there is a set format that is generally followed at all meetings. A typical meeting lasts about an hour and a half, and the number of people who attend varies— between ten and twenty-five as a rule. Each group has a chairperson, who changes every week, and that chairperson is usually a member who has volunteered.

Becoming a member of Al-Anon is as easy as attending your first meeting—but going to that first meeting may be one of the hardest things you have ever done. It need not be Let us consider some of the questions you may find yourself asking:

I'm shy around people—what can I do? Shyness is a *very* common human response—it is just that some people mask it better than others. Certainly if you are emerging from a hemmed-in relationship, feeling low and lonely, then of course you will feel somewhat nervous and uncomfortable. And why not? Your self-esteem has probably taken quite a beating. But do not worry. Many other members of Al-Anon have been there before you. They will recognize your feelings, and empathize. As a newcomer you will be warmly welcomed and immediately referred to as a member. You will be made to feel that you belong and can count on the support of the group.

Even with all this, however, it is best to begin by going with someone, especially a person who is familiar with the program. You may already know someone who belongs to Al-Anon and need only ask him or her to accompany you. If there is no one you know, you can call the Al-Anon central number in your area and arrange to have someone greet you or take you to a meeting. It is preferable to be accompanied to your first meeting because otherwise there is a temptation to isolate yourself and not become actively involved.

I hate speaking in public—suppose someone asks me to? Fear of speaking in public is one of the most widespread phobias in our society, and fortunately Al-Anon is perceptive enough to recognize this. While most meetings are open discussions, and each individual talks about his or her own feelings and experiences and says only what he or she wants to, no one is ever forced to speak. If you feel more comfortable listening, it is perfectly acceptable. (As the meeting wears on, however, you may find that you *want* to share your views.)

Discussions, it should be pointed out, are never confrontational. The objective is an exchange of views and a sharing of experiences and information. In this manner, members are able to gain new insights and learn from each other. The atmosphere is one of support, encouragement, and understanding.

What else can I expect? Occasionally a meeting may have one or several speakers who talk about a specific subject such as anger, depression, coping, and so forth. This is then followed by an open group discussion. When the meeting is over, many of the members sit around and discuss feelings or personal problems more informally Others may go out to socialize in a nearby restaurant

How much to join? There are no membership fees or dues or initiation rites

What are the rules? Rules are minimal and tend to be based on common sense. There is, however, a strong emphasis on confidentiality and anonymity. Last names are therefore not used, and what transpires at a meeting is not repeated outside. This assures privacy and reinforces a sense of trust within the group.

How should I dress? Al-Anon is thoroughly informal; there are far greater things at stake than whether you wear jeans or an A-line. Members of Al-Anon, though the fact is not always recognizable, have sprung out of almost everywhere you can imagine. Some have been reduced to ultimate poverty by alcoholism. Some have managed to hold mansions together in spite of alcoholism. Dress should be the least of your concerns.

Any final thoughts? Yes. When you finally do go, I strongly recom' mend that you attend meetings regularly for several months before making any final decision about whether or not this is for you. It is also important that you attend different Al-Anon groups in your area, since you may feel more comfortable with some groups than with others

WHAT AL-ANON CAN DO

Involvement in Al-Anon can be one of the most important steps you take in helping yourself to deal with the problems of living with an alcoholic. On the other hand, do not set yourself up for disappointment by creating unrealistic expectations. Al-Anon cannot stop your partner from drinking, nor can it really teach you how to get him to stop. If you go with the idea that this will inspire your partner to do something about his own problem or that your changing will make him want to change too, you may be missing the point.

Your decision to go to Al-Anon should be based on a desire to help *yourself*—to improve the quality of your life and diminish the emotional pain of living with an alcoholic. If it happens that in the course of your involvement your partner stops drinking or decides to obtain help through AA or professional treatment, then all the better

But whether he does or not, Al-Anon can and should be the beginning of a journey that takes you beyond a life based on mere survival and existence and into a world offering real choices and real options.

To begin with, Al-Anon provides a friendly and safe environment within which to learn more about the person you are and how your partner's alcoholism has affected you. You start to see that you are not alone in this world and that there are many women who have had similar experiences. As a result of this recognition, much of the shame and desperation that accompanies living with an alcoholic begins to fall away.

There is a sense of relief when you discover that the various feelings you have experienced are not unique to you, that many others have also felt the same emotions, and that these are normal and expected considering the circumstances in which you have been living. Hearing how other women have also tried to force their mates to stop drinking by screaming, arguing, begging, pleading, crying, and threatening allows you to realize that you are not mentally disturbed.

Listening to others, you may gain a deeper insight into what has happened to you and learn of the availability of alternatives that you may not previously have been aware of. Listening to others, especially those whose mates have already stopped drinking, will lead you to recognize that the cessation of drinking is not necessarily the end of the problem.

Al-Anon will help you focus on yourself rather than on the alcoholic. It will bring home the fact that while you cannot force him to stop drinking, you can certainly do something about the way his drinking affects you and the way in which you react to it—clearly, there is more to life than just reacting. You will begin to do things for yourself—not just things that are practical and survival-oriented, but things that are fun and pleasurable and personally rewarding. Taking control of your life means letting go: not trying to control his life—and not allowing him to control yours. It means paying attention to who you are and how you are with yourself and with the world around you.

Through Al-Anon you can learn about various community resources available to you and your family—how these may help you with specific problems, and how best to make use of these resources. Al-Anon also presents you with an opportunity to socialize and interact with others. Alcoholism may have resulted in the gradual drifting away of friends, or you may have become alienated from others in an effort to shield yourself from uncomfortable feelings.

Whatever the case, Al-Anon offers you a chance not just to go out to a meeting, but to develop a network of other women with whom you feel understood and accepted. When you are having a particularly bad day or a crisis arises, you have others to call on and know that you will be received with compassion.

Through Al-Anon you can regain much of the self-esteem and confidence that has been eroded over the years. You begin to develop a sense of self-worth. As you do, you find yourself able to talk more openly about your personal life and feelings. The change can serve as a model for your children. The fact that you are more at ease and relaxed will allow your children to feel more comfortable; it will open the door to a more honest sharing of feelings about what is really going on at home. You will not feel the need to pretend that everything is okay, or to blame everything that is not okay on the alcoholic. Your own example and improvement may be an incentive for your children to help themselves by joining self-help groups such as Alateen or ACOA.

Al-Anon also helps you to be more down-to-earth about your mate's possible recovery. You will not have unrealistic hopes about his stopping or unrealistic expectations that when he stops everything will be fine again. Most of all you will learn that *you* can change, whether he drinks or not.

SOME LIMITATIONS

No human being is perfect, and the institutions and programs created by humans are thus also imperfect. Though lack of perfection does not negate the importance or effectiveness of an institution, it should also not discourage us from trying to improve what we have created. There is no question that I respect Al-Anon greatly—if it did not exist, my own ability to work effectively with families of alcoholics would be severely hampered. Nonetheless, I have two concerns about the program.

My first concern is Al-Anon's apparent acceptance of the concept that alcoholism is a family disease. If we are to destigmatize alcoholism, we must also be prepared to remove the labels that misinform or misrepresent. The tendency to medicalize or mentalize all human behavior that is seen as inappropriate or ineffectual has opened the door to a labeling epidemic, especially in alcoholism, with terms such as "enabler," "codependent," and "paraalcoholic" flying fast and free.

The fact is, the concept of family disease is an outgrowth of the acceptance—legitimate as it may be—of alcoholism as a disease. Certainly there are some advantages to tagging the condition as a family disease. To take one example, the family may feel less guilty if they see their behavior in terms of an illness. To take another example, labeling certain behavior as an illness often results in professional help being made available to treat it, along with research funds to study it. But just because there are advantages in labeling something does not make it correct, especially if the label is inaccurate.

At some point we need to understand and accept that life is often filled with pain and seemingly unjust suffering. Such suffering can and does affect how we feel and behave. Most often we find ways to adjust to our suffering, and sometimes we adjust in ways that are self-limiting and self-defeating and that only serve to perpetuate our suffering rather than alleviate it. But does that mean we are sick?

The spouses and especially the children of Al-Anon do not need to be identified as "sick" just because they are emotionally involved with someone who is. I do not believe that people need to believe that they are sick in order to be willing to help themselves

VENTING YOUR ANGER

The second issue I would raise about Al-Anon is not so much a criticism as a cautionary note. While participation in this organization may be one of the most important moves a person can make in helping to deal with the emotional impact of living with an alcoholic, it is not always enough.

Al-Anon emphasizes the need to focus on oneself and not on the alcoholic. The message for the wife is that she is not responsible for her partner's drinking and cannot force him to stop if he is not ready to. Instead she is encouraged to concentrate on what she can do to change her own behavior and attitude. Discussing the behavior of the alcoholic—what he has done or is doing—is discouraged. Clearly, there are some good reasons for this approach.

By refraining from talking about the alcoholic and his behavior, Al-Anon has very correctly and cleverly avoided turning meetings into gripe sessions. Members need to learn that not everything can or should be blamed on the alcoholic, and by focusing on themselves they are able to develop constructive, creative strategies for making changes that will be beneficial to themselves and improve their situation.

Nonetheless, it is not always easy—in fact, sometimes it is quite impossible—for a person to get on with life without first taking care of unfinished business. It is certainly important that women recognize that they cannot control the drinker, but can control how they themselves behave. And letting go—detaching—is equally important. But for many women this is hard to do without first or simultaneously having the opportunity to vent their deep feelings of anger, frustration, hurt, and disappointment. They may need to talk these feelings out—maybe to cry, sob, or scream out in anger about all that the drinker and his drinking has put them through. It is one thing to face up to what needs to be done, or how one needs to change—but sometimes it is difficult to contain and repress profound feelings of anger and sadness. This is precisely where psychotherapy may be of great value.

PSYCHOTHERAPY

Though self-help programs such as Al-Anon can be very effective, they are not always enough. Sometimes professional intervention is necessary and beneficial. This does not mean that you are mentally sick, intellectually weak, psychologically disturbed, or emotionally unbalanced.

Unfortunately too many people think that this is precisely what going to therapy means, and as a result they shy away from speaking to a professional and thus miss out on assistance that might be extremely beneficial. To some extent, this is not at all surprising. Psychology and psychiatry often appear mysterious, if not intimidating. Numerous schools of thought, along with differing ideologies, theories, and approaches, make therapy appear much more complicated than it is.

In reality, psychotherapy is far simpler than the accumulation of all its theories might lead one to believe. Psychotherapy is not a happening or event that will result in magical discoveries or cures. Therapists are not gurus or individuals who are specially endowed, and they do not have the solutions to mankind's problems.

Good therapy will not teach you how to think, but it can help you to understand why you think the way you do. It will not teach you how to feel, but it can help you to be less afraid of feeling or expressing those feelings. It will not change the world in which you live, but it can help *you* to grow and change. As a result, the world often begins to look a little different, a little clearer, a little less intimidating, and a great deal easier to understand and handle.

In the process of gaining or regaining control over your own behavior you begin to feel less in need of trying to control those around you. Finally, as you grow and change, you realize that you need not apologize for having tried to help your partner, for having lied to his boss in order to protect yourself as well as your family, for having stayed with him because you thought you were doing the right thing or because you felt you had no alternative. Good therapy will help you realize that you are not sick or emotionally disturbed—just a very troubled person who may feel quite confused about all that has happened to you.

As the wife or companion of an alcoholic, you need an opportunity to feel validated. Years of screaming or crying or begging have often fallen on deaf ears—you need permission to "spill your guts" and you need a safe, warm, accepting place to do so. Chances are, you are filled with feelings of anger, hatred, pity, self-blame, guilt, and resentment. Without an opportunity to unload, there may be no possibility to move on. Failure to recognize this is a little like building a house without a foundation—while everything may look good, it will not last.

One of my clients put it very clearly when she wrote to me, "In retrospect I realize that a lot of what I had to say was petty, but I had to get the petty stuff out before I could get to the real feelings—and God, I was afraid of those feelings. I thought if I ever started I'd fall apart—I'd lose control, nobody would be able to put me back together. I don't know if I was more afraid that I would fall apart and go insane, or that you'd think I was crazy. But gradually I guess I was able to begin to trust you, that you wouldn't let me fall apart, that you wouldn't abandon me, that you understood—maybe most of all I felt you cared— and suddenly it was okay to cry, to scream, to just let go. What's amazing is that after those few weeks, I knew I was going to make it. I just knew that I could do what I had to do to make my life better."

CHOOSING A THERAPIST

If you have made the decision to go into therapy, the next issue is to find a therapist. Though most therapists are competent, they are not all equally skilled or gifted in the art of therapy. What is more, one who is very gifted may not necessarily be one you feel comfortable with and thus may not be appropriate for you. Choosing the "right" therapist is therefore of paramount importance.

Locating a therapist through the Yellow Pages is not the best method, though admittedly it may be the only method you have. A more effective way is to ask friends and relatives for recommendations. If you are in Al-Anon you might seek out the opinions of other members who have been in therapy. You might also consider discussing the question with your family physician.

The names that come up most often are probably your best bet. Next you may want to consider calling several of these therapists and setting up an appointment with each. After speaking or meeting with several therapists you should be in a position to make a decision. Generally, there are several issues to consider when making your evaluation:

WHAT YOU DO NOT WANT IN A THERAPIST

• You do not want a therapist who has little or no experience working with alcoholics and their families.

• You do not want a therapist who does not seem to know very much about Al-Anon and AA, or who appears skeptical about the value of these self-help groups.

• You do not want a therapist who focuses on your emotional conflicts and efforts to cope as manifestations of illness.

• You do not want a therapist who supports the belief that alcoholism is a family disease, or that wives of alcoholics are enablers or codependents.

• You do not want a therapist who tends to stereotype or categorize you (in other words, "wife of alcoholic") while ignoring the fact that you are a unique individual. You certainly do not want a therapist who appears to know your needs and understand your problems before he even knows you.

WHAT YOU DO WANT IN A THERAPIST

• You want a therapist who understands that alcoholics are not all the same, and that the experiences of their wives and children vary accordingly, and consequently so do their needs.

• You want a therapist who wants to understand you—that is, one who is genuinely interested in knowing what your experience has been, how you feel, how you see yourself and the world around you, and what your particular needs are.

• You want a therapist who will help you see why you are not to blame for your mate's drinking problem, while pointing out how you can help yourself in spite of what is going on around you.

• You want a therapist who is willing to confront your fears, but who is able to be warm and supportive—one who is also willing to give information and educate, not just treat.

In short, what you want is a well-rounded professional, a "real" human being, someone who is at once informed and knowledgeable, yet who is not so arrogant as to pretend to have all the answers or solutions. You want a person who is willing to get to know and understand you and your particular experience—your perception of yourself—and not one who appears to know about you almost instantly because of his or her preconceived ideas about alcoholism and alcoholics.

Key Points

• A wife's recovery should be independent of her partner's status. Whether he is drunk or sober, in one's life or out of it, it is essential to concentrate on dealing with one's own experience in the relationship.

• Chances are there is a backlog of anger, sadness, hurt, fear, and self-doubt built up. For a wife to effect a successful recovery, these feelings need to come to the surface.

• Joining a self-help group such as Al-Anon is a significant step in coming to grips with the experience of having lived with alcoholism—but this alone may not be enough. Therapy may also be necessary.

• Choosing the right therapist is of vital importance. It is essential to find one you feel comfortable with, who is knowledgeable about alcoholism and who regards you as an individual, not as a stereotype.

Voices: Christine, a wife

TEN GOOD YEARS

I joined Al-Anon at forty, after many years of frustration and upset about living with an alcoholic. I confess I didn't hold out much hope.

I didn't think anyone or anything could really help me. As it turns out, I couldn't have been more wrong.

One of the first things I learned is that helping yourself does not mean doing it all by yourself. It means reaching out to others who can help you to understand more clearly what has been happening to you. It means reaching out to people who can help you see that there are alternatives. It also means that you have to be willing to consider those alternatives and make use of resources that you previously ignored.

Yes, I was hurt and I felt angry, ashamed, guilty, mistrustful—just about all the emotions, I suppose, that come from living with an alcoholic. Yes, I was a victim—not necessarily of my husband's deliberate efforts to hurt me, but of his disease and disturbed behavior. But how much longer could I continue to go about life feeling resentment and self-pity, while pretending that I was really okay?

In many ways my situation reminded me of the game of hide-and-seek that children play. You've noticed how very young children are not especially good at it? They're not really sure how to hide themselves, so they simply stand in a corner or out in the open or behind a door—and they keep their eyes closed? If they can't see you, they believe that you can't see them. It's only when they get older that they realize the truth. I believe that by living with an alcoholic, I began to behave like that. It was as though I was returning to an infantile stage where I believed that by pretending I couldn't see what was going on, what was happening to me, nobody else could see it either—in other words, the situation didn't exist.

Just as my husband couldn't be blamed for having a disease, I couldn't be blamed for being the way I was. But I think an alcoholic can certainly be held responsible for not doing anything about his disease, and likewise I could be held responsible for not doing anything about being a victim in my own right. Denying that I had been affected did not mean that I hadn't been. Pretending that I was fine did not make me fine.

My feeling is that no matter what type of alcoholic you are involved with, it is impossible to go through the experience without feeling somehow hurt. My own husband, for example, was never a bad or belligerent drunk, and never unfaithful. Even so, I was all torn up inside. I think it must be pretty much the same for all wives of alcoholics. The emotional pain continues to affect the way you feel about yourself and how you act in certain situations. You may find having sexual relations impossible or difficult or simply unpleasurable. You may change your routine, the way you dress, the way you act with people, you may put the entire problem out of your mind. But it is part of you—and always will be. It is your baggage, your history.

There are people out there who have attempted to change history by simply denying it or trying to rewrite it. But that does not change history and will never make it other than it really was—it does not change reality. I guess my question for women married to alcoholics must be: How are you tuned into reality? Are you honest about it? To what extent has your relationship affected you and how does it continue to affect how you live out your life?

As for advice—if you want it—I would say get help as soon as possible. Al-Anon, therapy, whatever fits your needs—but do get help. You need to talk and share and even laugh at what you have been through. I know I did.

And I would add something more: joining an organization like Al-Anon, or going for counseling, does not mean that you and your husband are going to separate. I worried about that at one point, because I really did love my husband. What happened instead was that I actually began to see him in a better light, began to really— emotionally—grasp that he had a disease. Even so, I recognized that I had to get on with my own life.

Then another strange thing happened (though this is certainly not always the case): As I began to change, he began to take notice. At first he seemed to resent my going to Al-Anon, but eventually he was obliged to accept the fact. Then one day, very tearfully, almost like a child, he asked me for advice about what he could do to stop drinking. I could scarcely believe it, and my heart was almost breaking. I urged him to phone AA, and he did.

We had almost ten years together after that. He did marvelously well in the program, right up to the time of his death. Of course, I was saddened by his death, and I still am. But I'm also thankful for two things: the fact that I found Al-Anon in the first place and still have it as a resource—and the fact that we had those ten last years together. They were good ones.

Eleven

Family Therapy

If you ever need a helping hand, you'll find one at the
end of your arm.

—Yiddish proverb

It is true: The best help available is often the help we give ourselves.
Nonetheless, there are times when this alone is not enough—we
need to reach out. In this regard, family therapy is perhaps one of the
most effective tools available for unraveling the mess that living with
alcoholism usually produces. The reason? Not only does alcoholism
corrode the relationship between the drinker and his family, it also
deeply affects the relationship between mother and child, and
between child and child. In other words, virtually all aspects of family
interaction are short-circuited, and everyone needs assistance.

While self-help programs and general psychotherapy can go a long
way in aiding an individual to address his or her own problems and
initiate personal change and growth, they cannot directly focus on the
deeply troubled interpersonal relationships within the family. If the
family is assembled, however, individual members have an opportunity to begin to share with one another thoughts and feelings that
have been denied, repressed, and muffled for far too long.

During years of drinking, an alcoholic's wife and children learn to
adjust in order to survive. For many women, this means masking
their feelings, not just from outsiders but also from their family and

191

even themselves. For some, feeling anything at all is too painful and unbearable, so they choose to stop feeling altogether. They build walls to protect themselves from the uncontrollable bedlam around them—but in the end these walls serve only to make them prisoners of their marriage and of their family, and to alienate them from even their children, and vice versa. Though they survive, the cost is extortionate.

Therapy alone cannot break down these walls, but it can provide necessary support, understanding, and security so that the walls can begin coming down. The therapist can help a client realize that there is no longer a need to hide, that there is nothing to be ashamed of and nothing to fear, because the client is quite capable of dealing with what is at hand.

If you enter family therapy, as you gain courage and strength, you will begin to take down the walls around you. In turn, other members of the family will also feel able to come out of hiding. Together you can begin the task of rebuilding. You can begin to grow and change.

THE FAMILY EN ROUTE

I had continued to work with Melanie while she and her family were engaged in family therapy. My impression was that she was finding it to be a tough but positive experience. According to her, she had learned a great deal during the sessions, some of it not very pleasant, some of it quite painful. She explained that she had never realized the extent to which the children held her responsible for the situation at home: how much they had resented her outbursts of temper, her quarrels with Mike, her seemingly constant bad moods. In one session, Philip, the eldest, had wept, saying he wanted his "old" mum back, the one who smiled and laughed and loved him. His brother had said nothing; he had simply sobbed.

"As painful as this session was," Melanie said, "it helped me open my eyes, made me realize how much the children have been affected and that they were actually aware of everything that was going on. Until that time, I thought I had done an excellent job protecting them from what was happening. How blind I was!"

"The road to hell is paved with good intentions," I remarked casually.

"I agree—but at least you can sometimes come back. The good thing is that we've all begun to talk to each other again, even outside the family therapy sessions. Even Mike is beginning to open up."

"What do you mean, 'even'?"

"Well, at first, in the beginning, he didn't want to hear anything about the past. He said that the past was behind us, and now that he's no longer drinking we should all look to the future. But the therapist explained to Mike that it is essential for us to talk about the past, that it's important for the children and me to get our feelings out in the open instead of keeping them bottled up inside. She also said that it's very important for the whole family to know that Mike understands how much his drinking hurt and frightened us. Can you imagine what a difference that has made?"

I smiled. "I think I'm getting the picture."

Melanie then added that the family sessions had also helped her relationship with Mike:

"When Mike finally went into the treatment center I felt both relieved and anxious. I was glad he was doing something, but I was afraid of what would happen if he went back to drinking. You and Al-Anon helped me a lot in getting me to see that I have to live one day at a time and that I can't and don't need to control Mike—I just need to take care of who and how I am. I guess you know better than anyone how hard it was for me to let go."

I nodded, and Melanie continued: "Now in family therapy I'm learning the difference between taking care of and caring for. Mike doesn't need me to take care of him, and I don't want him to take care of me. But we've both been learning to show that we care *for* each other. We have a way to go—getting rid of bad habits isn't easy. But at least now there's hope."

As she finished speaking, Melanie's face grew gently radiant, and she smiled confidently. There was indeed hope, I thought.

WHAT ACTUALLY HAPPENS

When you enter family therapy, a new world may seem to unfold before you. It is not a new world, of course, but the way in which you see it will almost certainly be new. Family therapy enables you, your children, and your mate to begin to explore your feelings, and gradually to understand your own conflicts and ambivalences about yourself and each other. There is tremendous relief as you begin to realize that you are not alone—that you are not different, that you are not weird or abnormal, that you are not suffering from any mental disorder or family disease. Your feelings—be they guilt and self-blame, or anger and hate, or pity and concern, or fear and depression, or any of a number of other emotions—are all very normal, understandable reactions to a very sad, sometimes humiliating, and frequently frightening experience. Having bad feelings does not mean you are a bad person.

Family therapy will not only enable you to realize this, to come to terms with it within yourself, but more important it will give you an opportunity to share these feelings with other members of the family and at the same time to understand their perceptions and feelings about themselves and you. Often the best way to begin is with education. Videos, books, and lectures can help bring the family into focus about alcoholism and what it may have done to them. This is turn leads to an opening up and a sharing.

The process does not involve one or two sessions—it takes time, and it can also be very scary and painful. The road to growth and change is never an easy one. Exposing your feelings, your vulnerability, your fragility, is not simple. There will be tears and there will be anger. This unburdening of your soul, however, can bring a sense of relief that is not easily translated into words. You will feel the change in yourself, you will hear it in the voices of your husband and children, you will see it in their eyes—as I have seen it so often in other cases.

When this has been achieved, you are ready to let go of all those issues that you now realize you have no control over. You are ready to begin to work on the things you do have control over—your own growth and development—rather than organizing your entire life around your mate's alcoholism. At this point there is a sense of closeness, a sense of bonding between you and the children. There is also a greater sense of closeness to the alcoholic himself. You begin to see him as a human being with a very legitimate and serious problem.

Even so, though you feel closer, you also feel freer. As you begin to see the man and the disease as separate, you also begin to see that only he can do something about his disease—that it is not your responsibility, nor is it in your power to change him. You are now no longer an alcohostage. You are now able to begin to live, grow, and change. Nonetheless, sudden freedom after years of captivity takes some getting used to.

When the Jews were freed from bondage in Egypt, they did not go straight to the promised land. God made them wander through the desert for forty years, thus giving them an opportunity to adjust to freedom, to learn that freedom is itself a burden and a responsibility. He gave them time to learn to trust and to become a family, a nation. Until they had learned this lesson, they could not enter the promised land.

Though it will not take you forty years to adjust to freedom, to learn to trust, and to assume the responsibilities that come with freedom, it will take time and effort and energy. The cessation of drinking does not represent the promised land—it is only the termination of bondage and the beginning of the road to freedom.

WILL FAMILY THERAPY HELP MY ALCOHOLIC PARTNER?

As we have seen, many alcoholics assume that when they stop drinking everything will return to normal. They believe that their wives and children will be enthusiastic and supportive, and that the family will live happily ever after. Not only is this a very unrealistic expectation that can lead to disappointment, frustration, and tremendous resentment, it can also provide the basis for a relapse into drinking.

Involvement in family therapy can help the alcoholic recognize that his drinking was only part of the problem. His physical or emotional absenteeism, bizarre behavior, unpredictability, verbal abuse, and other shortcomings have left untold scars on his family. His wife and children cannot easily forget the pain of being rejected, nor the many incidents that left them feeling humiliated or frightened. The alcoholic needs to be made aware of all this, so that he has a context in which to understand the continued anger, fear, and lack of trust that the other family members have for him even after he has stopped drinking.

He must also realize that the family needs time, that he must be patient. They have had to wait for him to stop drinking; he may have to wait a while for them to begin to adjust to him as an abstinent, sober, and trustworthy individual. Too often the responsibility of being supportive and understanding is put on the shoulders of the family, and especially on the shoulders of the wife. It is extremely important that the alcoholic not be treated like a baby. His drinking has had consequences, and these do not get erased, forgotten, or forgiven by the mere act of not drinking.

In a sense, the alcoholic worked very hard at losing the trust of those who relied on him the most, and he must learn to accept that he will have to work equally hard at regaining that trust. This sounds unfair, and it probably is. The disease of alcoholism, however, has little to do with fairness. Family therapy gives the drinker an opportunity to understand this and to learn how to begin to work with his wife and children at rebuilding what has been destroyed. But family therapy will not be effective if the wife and children are not prepared to be open, maybe even brutally honest, about how they feel. This is not a punishment for the alcoholic, though it may initially appear that way. It is in fact an act of kindness and love.

If I, for example, am not honest with the people I love or who love me, if I do not share with them my feelings of anger and resentment, then no matter how hard I try I will never be able to love them as well as I should or would wish to. They in turn will sense that something is wrong, or that something is missing, and in the end the relationship will falter. Unless past business is attended to, it is very difficult to get on with the present and build for the future.

IS FAMILY THERAPY USEFUL IF A PARTNER IS STILL DRINKING?

The answer is, yes, most definitely. But whether or not the partner can or should be included in therapy sessions is another question.

If his drinking is severe and he would be coming to sessions in an intoxicated condition, then his inclusion would be largely pointless. In a drunken state it is improbable that he would benefit from what happens—in fact he might not even be able to recall the next day what was discussed. In addition, his behavior and attitude could be very disruptive. He could become loud, sarcastic, threatening, or belligerent. More than likely, this would be frustrating and frightening, and would discourage family members, especially children, from expressing their feelings or speaking freely.

In such situations, I believe family therapy should proceed without the participation of the alcoholic. There are those who might argue that the alcoholic should be included regardless of his state, and that it is the responsibility of the family to decide how to handle the situation. Although I see merit in this argument, I feel strongly that the therapist must set some ground rules and, in a sense, be an example to the family in demonstrating that life does not revolve around the alcoholic, and that life can go on even without the alcoholic.

On the other hand, if the alcoholic is prepared to attend therapy in at least a fairly sober state, then every effort should be made to include him.

WHAT IF THE PARTNER HAS STOPPED DRINKING?

Family therapy can be especially helpful when an alcoholic has stopped drinking or is attempting to do something about his problem—for example, when he has entered a treatment program, is in private therapy, or is attending AA.

Families tend to react in different ways to the cessation of drinking; individual members of the same family may also react very differently from one another. Sometimes the reaction is one of icy aloofness. The family seems to be saying, "So what—we've seen this before. Who cares?" There may be anger about all that has happened in the past, and an unwillingness to be supportive or understanding.

Other families may react in an opposite manner. They may feel elated, imagining that all their problems are over and that life is going to be wonderful.

A third reaction is a mixture of joy and anxiety. Family members feel glad that the alcoholic is finally doing something about his drinking, but they are not sure how to deal with it. They may be afraid to say or do anything that might upset him and make him drink again. They do not know if they can have guests over for dinner and serve drinks. They are not sure whether to go to social events where liquor will be available. They become overly protective of the alcoholic and try to do everything possible to keep him sober. Still other families might expect that once the alcoholic has stopped drinking, he will be exactly as he was before drinking was a problem.

The specific reaction of the family as well as their expectations can create new problems and deep disappointment. Family therapy, however, can help the entire family to become more realistic about their hopes, dreams, and expectations.

Families need to remember that alcoholism is a disease for which there is no cure—and therefore there is no certainty that the alcoholic will not relapse. They need to recognize that just as they could not make the alcoholic stop drinking, they also cannot make him drink. Most of all they need to realize that recovery from addiction is a process that takes time. Though the alcoholic has stopped drinking, he is not necessarily fully well. He may continue to be moody, irritable, and emotionally unstable for some time to come

The alcoholic must also face some realities. His drinking has resulted in consequences that cannot be easily forgotten. His behavior has caused a lot of hurt in others, and his reacceptance into the family is not automatically assured by the cessation of drinking.

Before the wife and children are able to begin to readjust to a life of abstinence, there may be a great deal of unfinished business—a torrent of feelings about the past that need to be expressed and acknowledged. It is essential for the alcoholic to realize that he cannot expect his wife or even the children to plan a future with him until the past and all the feelings attached to it have been resolved.

A WORD OF CAUTION

In spite of the enormous potential benefits from family therapy, it is not employed nearly enough as a means of helping families with an alcoholic member. Another problem is that when it is being employed, it is often more in the context of helping the alcoholic get sober and remain abstinent than in dealing with the specific needs of his wife and children. Indications are that alcoholism treatment centers do not usually offer services to the families of their alcoholic patients.

When individuals other than the alcoholic are included, it is usually the spouse, and that most often means the wife, while the children remain almost always excluded. But even when the wife takes part in her husband's treatment, the purpose of her participation is quite disturbing to me. Very often the sole reason for her being invited is to gain further information about the drinker, his style of drinking, his behavior, and the overall history of the problem.

This kind of information can be very helpful to clinical personnel who are treating the alcoholic, because it can help them gain a clearer picture of the degree and severity of the drinking problem. But how is this helpful to his wife? What about the way *she* has been affected, and what about the damage drinking has done to her and her relationship with the children? Most often, these issues are either ignored or addressed superficially, and the wife is reminded of her need to go to Al-Anon.

Another so-called benefit of family therapy is the tendency for alcoholics to stay longer in treatment and to complete their therapy when the spouse is involved in some capacity. Since there is an apparent positive relationship between completion of treatment and later abstinence, then obviously including the wife in any capacity is seen as helpful. But again, what about her specific needs?

I am not trying to diminish the importance of gaining information about the alcoholic by speaking to his wife, or to deny the fact that her participation may contribute toward further motivating him to help himself. But family therapy should not be used as the codeword to describe what in fact is most often the treatment of the alcoholic man and the involvement of his wife in some minor and vague capacity.

If the inclusion of a woman in her mate's treatment is helpful in his rehabilitation, then she should certainly be included. But that is *not* family therapy, nor should it be the major purpose of family therapy. As long as children are not included and as long as families are used as adjuncts to the treatment of the alcoholic, it is *not* family therapy—it is, at best, a misuse of the term.

Treatment has traditionally focused on the alcoholic. There are numerous approaches to treating alcoholism, with no indication that any one method is better than another. In the meanwhile, however, the family has remained very much neglected in terms of their own needs. Family therapy has the potential of overcoming the terrible neglect of spouses and children, but unfortunately it is often applied in a manner that really misses the point once again.

It would be unfair to say that only alcoholism treatment centers are responsible for this. Family service agencies have also failed to utilize this approach as a means of helping families with an alcoholic member. Very often, when families present themselves to a service agency—even when alcohol is a central problem in the family—they come in with specific problems other than the drinking. It may be the acting out of a child, an academic problem with a child, or a problem of family communication or interaction. In other words, though alcoholism may be a major problem in the family, the family does not present it as such. It is often in the hands of the clinician to identify the drinking problem—but the clinician frequently fails to do so because he or she is not looking for it, or because it is well masked.

At other times the drinking issue becomes apparent but is dealt with as if it were just one more family problem or even a secondary problem—a symptom of other family difficulties. Instead of addressing the drinking, it is either missed, ignored, or not seen as a primary item. Family therapy proceeds in an effort to improve one or a number of problems within the family, while ignoring this central concern. It becomes the mistaken belief or hope of all that by improving the communication between the parents, or by clarifying the behavioral problem of a child, an improvement in the alcoholic's drinking or even a complete cessation will be achieved.

This simply does not work. The alcoholic's drinking must be addressed first. Only when drinking is brought under control can other family problem areas be properly assessed, understood, and dealt with.

Sad to say, specialists in the treatment of alcoholism often lack the required training and knowledge about family dynamics and what family therapy is. Their major objective is the rehabilitation of the drinker. As a result the spouse and children do not get the attention they so badly need. On the other hand, specialists in family dynamics often lack the necessary training and experience in dealing with alcoholism and are thus unable to identify the existence of a drinking problem, or mistakenly believe that if they attempt to resolve other more easily treatable problems, the drinking will then resolve itself.

What is needed is much greater cooperation between these two specialties—either by working together, or by sharing information, or by upgrading their skills in each other's area of expertise. Then there can be a tremendous improvement in the treatment of families with an alcoholic member. Not only will the alcoholic be helped, but so too will the spouse and children.

Key Points

• Family therapy is an opportunity for each member of the family to share with others how he or she has been affected by the parent's alcoholism—something that many families have rarely done.

• When you discover that your experience is not unique, you begin to realize that you are not odd for feeling and thinking the way you do.

• When you unburden your feelings, you begin to experience a sense of relief—a greater sense of freedom, and a sense of closeness to other members of the family, including the alcoholic.

• The alcoholic's willingness or ability to attend sessions should not affect your decision to enter family therapy. He may continue to drink, but you and your children do not need to continue to suffer

Voices: Anonymous

WHO AM I?

I can be used if you know how. But use me with tender, loving care and I will bring joy and laughter. Abuse me and I will display my cunning and evil force to such magnitude that you will know that I am more powerful than all the armies of the world.

I have ruined the lives of more people than all the wars in history. I have caused millions of accidents and wrecked more cars and homes than all the floods, hurricanes, and tornadoes combined. I am the world's slyest thief. I steal billions of dollars each year. I find my victims among the rich and poor alike, the young and the old, the strong and especially the weak.

I have created lovers and torn them apart, at my will. I loom up to such great proportions that I cast black shadows over every field of labor.

I am relentless, insidious, and totally unpredictable. I bring sickness, poverty, and death. I give nothing and take all. I can be your worst, most dangerous enemy.

I am alcohol.

Twelve

Toward a Brighter Future

For all sad words of tongue or pen,
The saddest are these: "It might have been!"

—John Greenleaf Whittier, "Maud Muller"

The problems faced by women married to alcoholics are very real and at times overwhelming. Their efforts to rescue their mates from destruction while in the same breath attempting to ensure their own survival and that of their children are well seen in Melanie's dream about the whirlpool. Her dilemma—whether to turn her back on the man she loved or whether to try to rescue him and in the process possibly destroy herself and her children—is faced by many wives of alcoholics.

If she chooses to save herself and the children and her husband drowns, then she must later live with the question "What if? What if I had tried?" But even if she had attempted to get the lifeline to him and he had failed to grasp it, she would still be left with the question "What if I had tried a little longer? Maybe we could be a family today." Is this not the very question that drove Carla to near self-destruction?

For those not caught up in the heat of the crisis, the solution always appears so simple. Have we not all, at some time or other, observed a friend who is involved in a painful relationship and wondered to ourselves why he or she puts up with it? It is so much easier to know what to do when confronted with someone else's problem. When the problem is our own, however, deciding what to do or knowing what is best is suddenly much more complicated and frightening.

The wife of an alcoholic may attempt to rescue her mate because she feels it is the right thing to do, she may stay with him because she believes it is the best thing to do—yet these and many other choices she makes are labeled as enabling or as indicators of emotional illness. Scant attention is given to the fact that the choices and decisions made by wives of alcoholics are based on personal values, ethics, and morals.

WHAT CAN BE DONE?

One of the first things that needs to be done is to stop blaming women for their mates' alcoholism. For far too long, wives of alcoholics have been held responsible for a disease whose cause is unknown and for which there is no identifiable cure. Experts, having done their professional best, are allowed to fail; wives, however, are not so easily absolved.

As we have seen, theories of the past openly faulted such women for causing their husbands' alcoholism or accused them of deliberately choosing and needing to live with an alcoholic. While these particular theories are no longer popular, the attitudes of specialists and society in general have not changed much over the years.

We no longer say that women actually cause alcoholism, but we continue, implicitly and explicitly, to hold them accountable for aggravating the problem and for prolonging it. We no longer suggest that these women are innately disturbed and purposely choose an alcoholic mate, but we say that they become disturbed as a result of living with him, and that this mental and emotional "illness" they develop results in behavior that enables the alcoholic to continue to drink.

There are probably many responses to this inequity, but one that strikes me as particularly succinct can be found in an old proverb— that people who live in glass houses should not throw stones. We are all part of a society that is confused and ambivalent about our position on the use of drugs. While we appear to support concepts such as "Just Say No," we also tend to support the view that it is sometimes okay to just say yes. Alcohol is a mood- and mind-altering substance— it is a *drug* like any other drug, but it is treated very differently.

The attitude in much of society is that use of alcohol is a justifiable right. It is okay to be drunk if you are funny and entertaining, but not if you are belligerent and threatening. It is legal to be drunk and take a taxi, but illegal to be drunk and drive your own car. In short, it is okay to use this drug but not okay to get into trouble with it.

On the other hand, there are other drugs that are not acceptable, even if a person does not use them or is not under the influence, but simply has them in his or her possession. A gram of cocaine or hashish could land a person in jail, but a flask of rum would not. What makes this double standard even more difficult to comprehend is that the cost of alcohol abuse to the individual, the family, and society is greater than for all other drugs *combined*.

Much of this overall confusion is reflected in our attitude toward wives of alcoholics. A wife who does not allow a husband who does not appear to have a drinking problem to keep liquor at home or to drink at parties or occasionally with his buddies is said to be unreasonable or a prude. But the wife of a man who drinks himself into trouble, a wife who does not stop him from doing this, is said to be an enabler.

Are wives of alcoholics enablers any more than, say, the producers of the drug alcohol? Than those who spend fortunes promoting and marketing it? Than the governments that stand by idly while reaping tax revenues from the sale of alcohol? We are all part of a society that refuses to take a clear stand on the issue of drug and alcohol abuse. We are all affected by the negative consequences that stem from drinking, but we also enjoy the benefits. At the same time we have created a "police force" to monitor the situation. This force consists of wives and girlfriends.

These women are expected to be tolerant of their mates' use of alcohol and at the same time to be on the lookout for misuse or abuse. When a woman notices something going wrong, she is expected to bring the fact to the drinker's attention and take whatever action is necessary and reasonable to control his problem, including motivating him to accept treatment and supporting him in therapy and afterward. In the process she runs the risk of being seen as an accomplice—a coalcoholic or codependent. She is said to be as disturbed as he is and suffering from an illness similar to his

There is a quote by the eighteenth-century French dramatist Nicolas Chamfort which goes: "We leave unmolested those who set fire to the house, and prosecute those who sound the alarm."

Where wives of alcoholics are concerned, it might be said that we also prosecute those who attempt to put out the fire

WHAT WOMEN NEED TO KNOW

Women involved with drinkers need to know more about what alcoholism is and how to recognize the signs and symptoms. There are so many definitions that it is difficult even for professionals to identify an alcoholic. Many women who suspect an alcoholism problem in their mate are manipulated into believing that it is either normal drinking or a passing phase. Women need to know that while alcoholism is regarded as an incurable disease, it can be successfully controlled with proper attention and appropriate treatment. They also need to know that they are not at fault, that they did not cause the problem, and that they need not blame themselves or accept the accusations of the alcoholic. Many women feel responsible, which leads to feelings of guilt and an overwhelming sense of shame and failure.

Women also need to know that there are services and resources available where they can receive guidance, understanding, and support for themselves and their children, and that there are treatment facilities available that can help the alcoholic husband. They need to know that they are not responsible for the alcoholic's rehabilitation and that they cannot really force him to stop drinking if he does not want to. Falsely believing that they can bring about change in their husbands leads many wives into months and years of unnecessary suffering because they delay seeking assistance

Women also need to know that the way they feel and the ways they have tried to cope are not indications of sickness or disturbance. The experience of living with an alcoholic is tremendously stressful and often not very different from that of being a hostage. A wife under such circumstances needs to know that she is a normal human being who is going through—or may already have been through—an extremely depressing, demoralizing, or frightening situation over which she is powerless. She needs to know that the mere fact she has survived says a great deal about her strength and courage.

Women should also know that a mate's cessation of drinking will not automatically make everything better, that this is but the first step in a long process Many women feel guilt-ridden and ashamed feel that there is something terribly wrong with them because they are unable to feel overjoyed and excited after a mate finally stops drinking. These women need to be helped to understand that many of the problems caused by alcoholism continue after drinking has stopped and that many of the losses incurred over years of intoxication will take time to even out—while some can never even out. In addition, there are often memories of horrible fights and humiliating incidents, and dreams and nightmares that keep recurring and affecting the way they feel. It will take patience and sometimes therapy to overcome these haunting experiences. The cessation of drinking does not remove the memories of those painful days, and it can take time before a wife is ready to trust again and to interact in an open and intimate way.

Finally, women need to know and understand that whatever they did to combat their mate's alcoholism, they did out of necessity, out of desire to survive and to protect their family from physical and emotional harm and societal gossip and shame, even though these actions may not always have been successful or even appropriate. They need to know that many so-called experts are wrong almost as often as they are right. And they need to know that some specialists hold views that are far from correct and may even be harmful.

WHAT CAN PROFESSIONALS DO?

Just about all of us in the professional field could benefit by reevaluating our current assumptions about wives of alcoholics. To offer support rather than blame, no matter how subtle or tacit, should be a priority. The notion that alcoholism is a family disease also needs serious rethinking. Though there may be practical advantages to considering it a disease, these should be carefully weighed against the obvious disadvantages of further stigmatizing these women and children. Alcoholism most certainly is a family problem, but those who live with the alcoholic are not themselves sick.

It would also be desirable that we make a greater effort to work more closely with self-help programs such as Al-Anon, Alateen, ACOA, and AA. Unfortunately some professionals feel they need to compete with these organizations, and thus either diminish their importance or neglect to use them as referrals. If more professionals took the time to attend some of the meetings and familiarize themselves with the literature they might feel differently.

There is also a great need for further research into families of alcoholics. Though much more attention is being given in this area, our knowledge of the impact of alcoholism on wives, husbands, and children of alcoholics is still relatively thin. At present there is a tendency to describe the effects and coping styles of families as if they were all more or less the same, yet families are not all affected in the same way and their experiences may differ considerably from one to another.

Specific treatment programs need to be developed for families, just as they currently exist for the alcoholic. In addition, since the needs of families may differ, a variety of services should be developed or expanded. Some spouses and children may require formal therapy, others will do well in self-help programs. Some women will need financial assistance, vocational training, or help with infants while others may require protection, emergency shelter, or halfway houses

Considerably more effort is also needed in the area of information and education. Lack of awareness of available resources is part of the reason spouses and children are not receiving much-needed assistance. This can be accomplished: by expanded use of public media, by more emphasis on the problems of alcoholism in television soap operas and children's programs, by offering training courses to teachers and school counselors so that they are better able to identify troubled children and better able to open up discussion with them, and by funneling literature concerning alcoholism through company-based employee assistance programs.

Much progress is taking place. But more *can* be done, more *needs* to be done.

HISTORY REPEATS

I still hear from Carla from time to time. She calls to say hello, to touch base, to let me know how her life is going. Naturally, I am pleased to hear from her, to hear about her progress. Most recently, several months ago, she telephoned to say that she had just become engaged. She sounded happy and positive, and—laughing—she described herself as a far cry from the woman I had met on that winter day so long ago.

After I hung up, I found myself thinking back. In those days she had been downing pills and drinking abusively. By ingesting these substances for reasons of escapism, she had been well on the way to developing a serious dependency. She had thought there was no hope, no point, but time and effort had reversed all of that. Now she was engaged, her children were doing well, her laughter was real and wholesome. I felt happy for her and gratified to have been a part of her recovery

Carla came to my mind again a few weeks later when a new client, a woman in her forties, a mother of five children, came to see me. Like so many clients who have sat in front of me, she was wondering where she had gone wrong. Her husband had recently been fired from his job following numerous warnings about his drinking. The day after his dismissal he had gone into the basement and had hanged himself.

We spoke long and deep about what she had been through, and clearly her world looked impossible at that moment. She felt friendless and alone, and abandoned and betrayed. As we made an appointment to meet again, I asked if she would consider talking to someone from Al-Anon. Once I had given her a brief explanation, she consented, and shortly after she left, I consulted my address book and telephoned Carla. Her answer was as I expected—she had a good idea of what the woman was going through, and she would invite her to a meeting that very evening.

UPS AND DOWNS

Melanie also calls occasionally to touch base. Some time ago she telephoned to tell me that Mike was about to receive his anniversary cake at AA—three years of steady sobriety. It was clear that she was proud, and I relayed my congratulations to both of them.

Melanie usually sums up her life as pretty good. "Like any couple, we have our ups and downs," she once said, "but at least the problems are not about alcoholism anymore. We have our differences and sometimes we argue, but we also know how to resolve our differences now."

Every Christmas I receive a card from her, and there is always some sort of quip or punch line. This past Christmas, the card read: "Morris, Just wanted to say thanks for helping me believe in Santa again." I smiled when I read this.

But it was her closing line that got me.

It said: "Things do get better."

Well, I guess sometimes they really do.

Recommended Readings

Though I do not necessarily support the views of some of the following authors, I consider these works highly informative.

GENERAL BOOKS

The Road Less Traveled
M. Scott Peck, M.D.
New York: Touchstone Books, Simon & Schuster, 1978

The Myth of Women's Masochism
Paula J. Caplan, Ph.D.
New York: Signet Books, 1985

When Talk Is Not Cheap
Mandy Aftel, M.A., M.F.C.C., and Robin Tolmach Lakoff, Ph.D.
New York: Warner Books, 1985

Necessary Losses
Judith Viorst
New York: Simon & Schuster, 1986

Living with Chronic Illness
Cheri Register
New York: The Tree Press, 1987

BOOKS ABOUT FAMILIES AND SPOUSES OF ALCOHOLICS

Power to Change
Edward Kaufman, ed.
New York: Gardner Press, 1984

Diagnosing and Treating Co-dependence
Timmen L. Cermak, M.D.
Minneapolis: Johnson Institute Books, 1986

Codependent No More
Melody Beattie
New York: Harper/Hazelden, 1987

Taking Charge
Stephen E. Schlesenger, Ph.D., and Lawrence K. Hoberg, Ph.D.
New York: Simon & Schuster, 1988

BOOKS ABOUT CHILDREN AND ADULT CHILDREN OF ALCOHOLICS

Keeping Promises
Kay Marie Porterfield
New York: Harper/Hazelden, 1984

Providing Care for Children of Alcoholics
David C. Lewis, M.D., ed., and Carol N. Williams, Ph.D.
Pompano Beach, Fla.: Health Communications, 1986

The Forgotten Children
R. Margaret Cork
New York: PaperJacks, 1969

Adult Children of Alcoholics
Janet Geringer Woititz, Ed.D.
Pompano Beach, Fla.: Health Communications, 1983

Children of Alcoholics
Robert J. Ackerman
Holmes Beach, Fla.: Learning Publications, 1983

Let Go and Grow
Robert J. Ackerman
Pompano Beach, Fla.: Health Communications, 1987

Broken Bottles, Broken Dreams
Charles Deutsch
New York: Teachers College Press, Columbia University, 1982

It Will Never Happen to Me
Claudia Black, Ph.D., M.S.W.
New York: Ballantine Books, 1981

BOOKS ABOUT ALCOHOLICS

The Natural History of Alcoholism
George E. Vaillant
Cambridge, Mass.: Harvard University Press, 1983

The A.A. Experience
Milton A. Maxwell
New York: McGraw-Hill, 1984

I'll Quit Tomorrow
Vernon E. Johnson
New York: Harper & Row, 1973

The Courage to Change
Denis Wholey
New York: Warner Books, 1984

Under the Influence
Dr. James R. Milam and Katherine Ketcham
New York: Bantam Books, 1981

To the Reader: An Invitation

Have you had an experience with alcoholism that you would like to share? If so, the authors would appreciate hearing from you, since there is a possibility that we will be publishing a follow-up work to this volume, one that deals with letters from individuals who have been involved with alcoholics. Anonymity, of course, will be fully respected. Please write to: *Women*, % P.O. Box 119 St-Philippe LaPrairie, Quebec, Canada J0L 2K0